BEGINNERS' GUIDE TO THE FED

Why it is Unique on our Planet

YITZHAK Q. ROSENTHAL

***Beginners' Guide to the FED:
Why it is Unique on our Planet***

by Y.Q. Rosenthal

ISBN 978-1-64550-011-7 (Paperback)

CONTENTS

This book is part of a 2019 decalogue consisting of

- Sign of Times: Music Anthology and Lyric Analysis
- Hollywood Misogyny
- Beginners' Guide to the FED:
  Why it is Unique on our Planet
- The Kennedy Kurse: Four Obvious Konnektions
- Manichaeism and Satanic Child Abuse
- Progressive Intolerance: Last Stop Before Hitler
- Patriotic Ingenuousness
- Deism versus Theism:
  2-7 in the Scientific Arena of the 20th Century
- Feminine Feminist: A Missing Link Eluding Discovery
- The Snake: Three Millennia of Anti-Semitism

Dedicated to All
who Suffered its Terror

INTRODUCTION
"I have proved Marx wrong"

These words were once written by Henry Ford sr., founder of Ford Motors Company. The context was the end of the 19th century in the US, with financial panics occurring at the rate of collapsing domino rows. What he meant by his statement, was that a free market system with capitalist enterprises was able to provide a tremendous amount of jobs. Moreover, Ford managed to imply his employees in such a way that they all loved the Company. His claim was perfectly sound. He revealed that Marx was basically a pessimist, favoring uprisings and chaos. Marx certainly would have won a Nobel prize, had he lived a bit later. All Nobel prizes awarded since 1969 are indeed of a neo-Marxist nature: that is, they all feign that the US has a free market, and that the FED is governmental institute, in the sense that only the Government decides what happens.

In contrast to the economic theories of Nobel prize winners, in this book the author takes a deeper look at the US Federal Reserve System (FRS), better known as the FED. This study is particularly concerned with the abnormality that a single banking mafia controls all of the FED, and through the FED, the semi-democratically chosen American President. Obviously, in order to understand the economic arguments one needs to master at least the basic terminology of macroeconomics. With this purpose in mind I wrote the first appendix, which is an introduction to macroeconomics for beginners, followed by some articles meant for advanced readers. The three chapters are dedicated to the following topics:

Chapter 1 copies the Wikipedia site description of the FED: that means, it tells one exactly how the FED wants to be conceived by US citizens.

Chapter 2 presents all well-documented and hardly discussed historical facts. They illustrate the abnormality of US recessions in history, the growth of the national debt, the unreasonable discontinuation of the publication of the M3 money supply figures, the bias of the economic "Nobel Prizes", the extraordinary coincidence of US Presidential assassinations with a strong financial motive, and the total isolation of the dollar with respect to all other currencies.

Chapter 3 gives the straightforward solution to all questions arising in chapter 2.

Due to the extremely compelling character of the proof that something is totally wrong with the FED, I hereby reproduce the decisive graph from section 2.2, referring to the ever increasing US National Debt over Gross Domestic Product ratio. The graph shows periods of debt accrual (dark grey areas below the ND/GDP curves) and of debt redemption in the subsequent years (light grey areas below the ND/GDP curves). From a fit of decreasing exponentials to the raw data (continuous lines through the discrete data points, starting in the year 1870), one concludes that, in periods free of wars and recessions, all debt was always redeemed within a period of 10 to 20 years. The essential anomaly is that, in order to fit the measured data, one needs to add an *increasing exponential*.

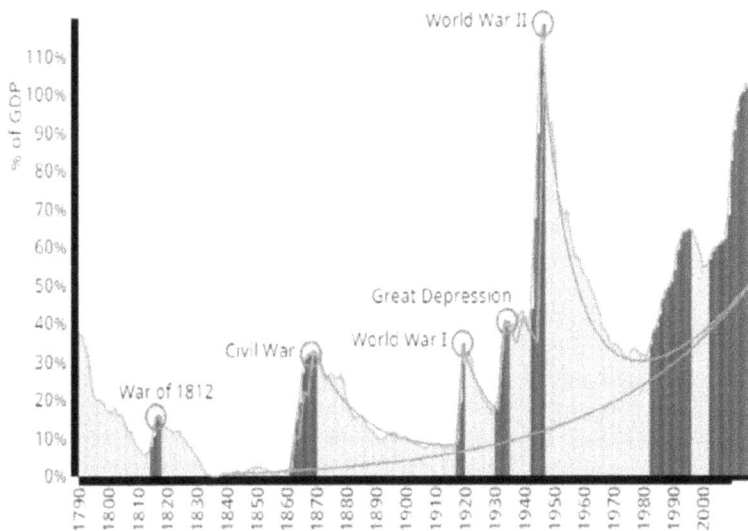

The discrete grey line starting in the year 1790 shows the "data" (the recorded national debt as a percentage of GDP). The smooth grey line, starting at the American Civil War, is the sum of the single exponentially increasing line, and a five decreasing exponentials. The latter have decay times of about 15 years, the recovery time of the American economy. The big question arises: **Why can the US not redeem the exponentially increasing debt component? Apparently, there is an inherent mechanism in the American law that nobody knows of. This is a clear pointer to an obscure role of the FED.**

As a rule, for better legibility, all quoted passages are written in a different font as compared to the standard.

CHAPTER I
How the FED Profiles Itself

This chapter reproduces a Wikipedia page accorded by the FED.[1] The article was written July 1st, 2014, whence minor details (like the names of bank presidents) might be outdated. All footnotes reflect the author's view, not that of the FED.

1.1 Composition

The Federal Reserve System is composed of five parts:

- The (...) Federal Reserve Board, an independent federal government agency located in Washington, D.C.

---

1 https://en.wikipedia.org/wiki/Structure_of_the_Federal _Reserve_System

- The Federal Open Market Committee (FOMC), composed of the seven members of the Federal Reserve Board and five of the twelve Federal Reserve Bank presidents, which oversees open market operations, the principal tool of U.S. monetary policy
- Twelve regional Federal Reserve Banks located in major cities throughout the nation (...)
- Numerous other private U.S. member banks (...)
- Various advisory councils

According to the board of governors of the Federal Reserve, "It is not 'owned' by anyone and is 'not a private, profit-making institution'. Instead, it is an independent entity within the government, having both public purposes and private aspects." The U.S. Government does not own shares in the Federal Reserve System or its component banks, but does receive all of the system's annual profits after a statutory dividend of 6% on their capital investment is paid to member banks and a capital account surplus is maintained. The government also exercises some control over the Federal Reserve by appointing and setting the salaries of the system's highest-level employees.

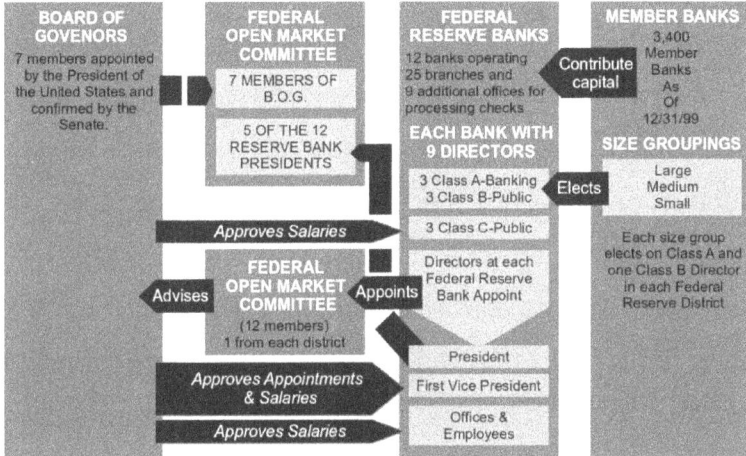

BOARD OF GOVENORS	FEDERAL OPEN MARKET COMMITTEE	FEDERAL RESERVE BANKS	MEMBER BANKS
7 members appointed by the President of the United States and confirmed by the Senate.	7 MEMBERS OF B.O.G.	12 banks operating 25 branches and 9 additional offices for processing checks	3,400 Member Banks As Of 12/31/99

Contribute capital

| | 5 OF THE 12 RESERVE BANK PRESIDENTS | EACH BANK WITH 9 DIRECTORS | SIZE GROUPINGS |

Approves Salaries

3 Class A-Banking
3 Class B-Public   Elects
3 Class C-Public

Large
Medium
Small

Each size group elects on Class A and one Class B Director in each Federal Reserve District

Advises — FEDERAL OPEN MARKET COMMITTEE (12 members) 1 from each district — Appoints — Directors at each Federal Reserve Bank Appoint

Approves Appointments & Salaries

President
First Vice President

Approves Salaries

Offices & Employees

Organization of the Federal Reserve System

The division of the responsibilities of a central bank into several separate and independent parts, some private and some public, results in a structure that is considered unique among central banks. It is also unusual in that an entity outside of the central bank – the U.S. Department of the Treasury – creates the currency used.

1.2 Independent within government

This often cited[2] research published by Alesina and
Summers (1993) is used to show why it is important
for a nation's central bank (*i.e.*-monetary authority) to
have a high level of independence. This chart shows a
clear trend towards a lower inflation rate as the
independence of the central bank increases. The
generally agreed upon reason independence leads to
lower inflation is that politicians have a tendency to
create too much money if given the opportunity to do
it. The Federal Reserve System in the United States
is generally regarded as one of the more independent
central banks.[3]

---

2   That a scientific article is often cited is merely indicative, though
     not a warrant of its quality.
3   The Federal Reserve System is by no dictionary a "central bank".
     Quite to the contrary, it is privately owned by American law,
     whence it is strictly independent of the President, his
     government, House, and Senate. The "average index of central
     bank independence" is in principle a relevant quantity. However,
     its definition in the scientific paper is evidently manipulated.
     What is the use of presenting a chart showing a trend using only
     14 countries? Were the authors too lazy to include African or
     Asian countries? Or are they not serious enough? The nice trend
     is entirely due to the obvious lack of statistics. Moreover, the

Central Bank Independence vs. Average Inflation

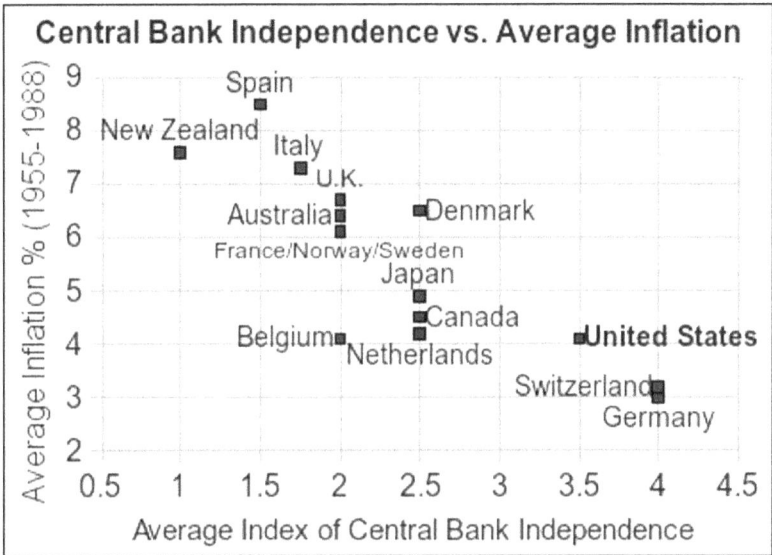

Inflation versus central bank independence⁴

independence of the US "central bank" is clearly flawed: it was simply assigned an independence number which put it right on top of the linear trend. If by "central bank" one understands the US National Bank (), the independence is significantly overestimated: it should be close to unity, like in New Zealand, thereby replacing the "linear trend" by arbitrary scatter. On the other hand, if by "central bank" one understands the Federal Reserve System, its independence is enormously underestimated. Neither Switzerland nor Germany have a US-like private FED, and therefore should have a lower independence number than any country with a FED-like construction. To date, there exists one only. EZ-puppets Macron (President of France) and Merkel (Chancellor of Germany) are presently fighting for a European FED.

4 The definition of the central bank independence does not have a maximum value. I still need to meet the first reader of Wikipedia

The Federal Reserve System is an independent government institution that has private aspects. The System is not a private organization and does not operate for the purpose of making a profit The stocks of the regional federal reserve banks are owned by the banks operating within that region and which are part of the system.

The System derives its authority and public purpose from the Federal Reserve Act passed by Congress in 1913. As an independent institution, the Federal Reserve System has the authority to act on its own without prior approval from Congress or the President. The members of its Board of Governors are appointed for long, staggered terms, limiting the influence of day-to-day political considerations. The Federal Reserve System's unique structure also provides internal checks and balances, ensuring that its decisions and operations are not dominated by any one part of the system. It also generates revenue independently without need for Congressional funding.

---

who thinks that, by making a central bank 100% independent of the government, the country in question automatically obtains deflation instead of inflation.

Congressional oversight and statutes, which can alter the Fed's responsibilities and control, allow the government to keep the Federal Reserve System in check. Since the System was designed to be independent while also remaining within the government of the United States, it is often said to be "independent within the government".

The twelve Federal Reserve banks provide the financial means to operate the Federal Reserve System. Each reserve bank is organized much like a private corporation so that it can provide the necessary revenue to cover operational expenses and implement the demands of the board. A member bank is a privately owned bank that must buy an amount equal to 3% of its combined capital and surplus of stock in the Reserve Bank within its region of the Federal Reserve System. This stock "may not be sold, traded, or pledged as security for a loan" and all member banks receive a 6% annual dividend. No stock in any Federal Reserve Bank has ever been sold to the public, to foreigners, or to any non-bank U.S. firm. These member banks must maintain fractional reserves either as vault currency or on account at its Reserve Bank. As of October 2008, the Federal

Reserve has paid interest to banks' holdings in Reserve Banks' accounts. The dividends paid by the Federal Reserve Banks to member banks are considered partial compensation for the lack of interest paid on the required reserves. All profit after expenses is returned to the U.S. Treasury or contributed to the surplus capital of the Federal Reserve Banks. Since shares in ownership of the Federal Reserve Banks are redeemable only at par, the nominal "owners" do not benefit from this surplus capital. In 2010, the Federal Reserve System contributed $79 billion to the U.S. Treasury.

1.3 Board of Governors

The seven-member Board of Governors is the main governing body of the Federal Reserve System. It is charged with overseeing the 12 District Reserve Banks and with helping implement national monetary policy. Governors are appointed by the President of the United States and confirmed by the Senate for staggered, 14-year terms. By law, the appointments must yield a "fair representation of the financial, agricultural, industrial, and commercial interests and geographical divisions of the country", and as stipulated in the Banking Act of 1935, the Chairman and Vice Chairman of the Board are two of seven members of the Board of Governors who are appointed by the President from among the sitting Governors. As an independent federal government agency, the Board of Governors does not receive funding from Congress, and the terms of the seven members of the Board span multiple presidential and congressional terms. Once a member of the Board of Governors is appointed by the president, he or she functions mostly independently. The Board is required to make an annual report of operations to the Speaker of the U.S. House of Representatives. It also supervises and regulates the operations of the Federal Reserve Banks, and the U.S. banking system in general.

Membership is by statute limited in term, and a member that has served for a full 14-year term is not eligible for reappointment. There are numerous occasions where an individual was appointed to serve the remainder of another member's uncompleted term, and has been reappointed to serve a full 14-year term. Since "upon the expiration of their terms of office, members of the Board shall continue to serve until their successors are appointed and have qualified", it is possible for a member to serve for significantly longer than a full term of 14 years. The law provides for the removal of a member of the Board by the President "for cause".

1.4 Federal Open Market Committee

The Federal Open Market Committee (FOMC) created under 12 U.S.C. § 263 comprises the seven members of the board of governors and five representatives selected from the regional Federal Reserve Banks. The FOMC is charged under law with overseeing open market operations, the principal tool of national monetary policy. These operations affect the amount of Federal Reserve balances available to depository institutions, thereby influencing overall monetary and credit conditions. The FOMC also directs operations undertaken by the Federal Reserve in foreign exchange markets. The representative from the Second District, New York, is a permanent member, while the rest of the banks rotate at two- and three-year intervals.

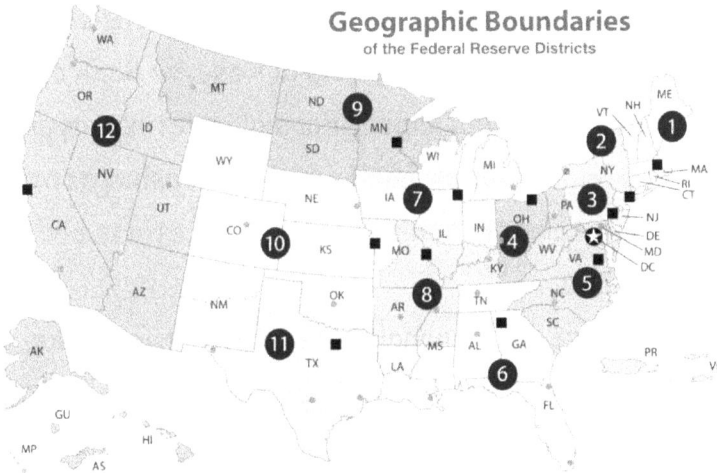

Geographic Boundaries
of the Federal Reserve Districts

Map of the twelve Federal Reserve Districts (black circles with white number), with the twelve Federal Reserve Banks marked as black squares, and all Branches within each district (24 total) marked as grey circles. The Washington DC Headquarters is marked with a star.

All the presidents participate in FOMC discussions, contributing to the committee's assessment of the economy and of policy options, but only the five presidents who are committee members vote on policy decisions. The FOMC, under law, determines its own internal organization and by tradition elects the Chairman of the Board of Governors as its chairman and the president of the Federal Reserve Bank of New York as its vice chairman. Formal meetings typically are held eight times each year in Washington, D.C. Telephone consultations and other meetings are held when needed.

There are 12 regional Federal Reserve Banks, not to be confused with the "member banks", with 25 branches, which serve as the operating arms of the system. Each Federal Reserve Bank is subject to oversight by the Board of Governors. Each Federal Reserve Bank has a board of directors, whose members work closely with their Reserve Bank president to provide grassroots economic information and input on management and monetary policy decisions. These boards are drawn from the general public and the banking community and oversee the activities of the organization. They also appoint the presidents of the Reserve Banks, subject to the approval of the Board of Governors. A Reserve Bank board consist of nine members: six serving as representatives of nonbanking enterprises and public, and three as representatives of banking. Each Federal Reserve branch office has its own board of directors, composed of three to seven members, that provides vital information concerning the regional economy.

1.5 Legal status

The Reserve Banks opened for business on November 16, 1914. Federal Reserve Notes were created as part of the legislation to provide a supply of currency. The notes were to be issued to the Reserve Banks for subsequent transmittal to banking institutions. The various components of the Federal Reserve System have differing legal statuses.

Bank		President
Boston	A 1	Eric S. Rosengren
New York City	B 2	William C. Dudley
Philadelphia	C 3	Patrick T. Harker
Cleveland	D 4	Loretta J. Mester
Richmond	E 5	Vacant
Atlanta	F 6	Raphael Bostic
Chicago	G 7	Charles L. Evans
St Louis	H 8	James B. Bullard
Minneapolis	I 9	Neel Kashkari
Kansas City	J 10	Esther George
Dallas	K 11	Robert Steven Kaplan
San Francisco	L 12	John C. Williams

The Federal Reserve Districts along with their President, and identifying letter and number

The Federal Reserve Banks have an intermediate legal status, with some features of private corporations and some features of public federal agencies. The United States has an interest in the Federal Reserve Banks as tax-exempt federally created instrumentalities whose profits belong to the federal government, but this interest is not proprietary. Each member bank (commercial banks in the Federal Reserve district) owns a nonnegotiable share of stock in its regional Federal Reserve Bank. However, holding Federal Reserve Bank stock is unlike owning stock in a publicly traded company. The charter of each Federal Reserve Bank is established by law and cannot be altered by the member banks. Federal Reserve Bank stock cannot be sold or traded, and member banks do not control the Federal Reserve Bank as a result of owning this stock. They do, however, elect six of the nine members of the Federal Reserve Banks' boards of directors. In Lewis v. United States, the United States Court of Appeals for the Ninth Circuit stated that: "The Reserve Banks are not federal instrumentalities for purposes of the FTCA [the Federal Tort Claims Act], but are independent, privately owned and locally controlled corporations." The opinion went on to say, however, that: "The Reserve Banks have properly been held to be federal instrumentalities for some purposes." Another relevant decision is Scott v. Federal Reserve Bank of Kansas City, in which the distinction is made between Federal Reserve Banks, which are federally created instrumentalities, and the Board of Governors, which is a federal agency.

CHAPTER 2
The Main Issues

2.1 History of Recessions

There have been as many as 47 recessions in the United States dating back to the Articles of Confederation.[5] Recession unemployment waves were much higher before the Great Depression (1929-1930) than ever after, excluding of course the two world wars. Factors like agricultural production, industrial production, consumption, business investment, and the health of the banking industry are often mentioned as causes of a recession. They are definitely not causes, but merely symptoms, the most indicative of which is the unemployment dip.

The unofficial beginning and ending dates of recessions in the United States have been defined by the National Bureau of Economic Research (NBER), an American private nonprofit research organization. I collected their tables in the online-available appendices.

---

5 https://en.wikipedia.org/wiki/List_of_recessions_in_the_ United_States. Most of the material in this chapter is taken from that website. Due to some deletions and additions of mine, however, the intention of the writer of that webpage has turned upside down.

The NBER defines a recession as "a significant decline in economic activity spread across the economy, lasting more than half a year, normally visible in real gross domestic product (GDP), real income, unemployment, industrial production, and wholesale-retail sales".

In the 19th century, recessions frequently coincided with financial crises, that is, with basic problems in the banking system. The occurrence of 18th and 19th century recessions is often an academic exercise in pattern recognition, due to the lack of reliable hard economic numbers. These patterns are due to quite ordinary cause-effect relationships. For example, an *agricultural* cause of a strong recession is the absence of food, which can be due to failed harvests as a consequence of sustained bad weather throughout a country. Likewise, a *financial* cause of a recession is the sudden loss in people's confidence concerning all banks' "solvency", that is, their ability to pay out the people's savings. In case such a financial cause is one of the many, the financial cause could be *morally neutral*. In case the financial cause is the first one, coinciding with a concerted decision of a sufficiently influential group of bankers, the cause is *morally wrong*: it is equal to theft. Bankers simply rob all ordinary people's savings by having their banks go bankrupt. What is left is a chicken without feathers. People have to sell their houses, or take heavy mortgages. After a year of banking panic and unemployment, the same banks, housed in the same buildings, change names and take up business like before, though this time, holding huge financial claims on the citizens.

So how can influential bankers provoke a recession? Assume those bankers owed their account holders a large sum of savings. The bankers could decide to invest all that money in a single big operation, like the construction of nation-wide engine-building factories. Before the recession actually occurs, those bankers send out some phony signals to society, like a series of articles in the most-read newspapers, pointing at some fake cause of a possible solvency dip of some important banks. That provokes a run on the banks by people trying to get back their savings. After the tenth pay-out, the eleventh account holder (in a queue of thousands of them) hears that the bank is out of money, due to that phony reason. The poor, mostly ignorant, account holders believe the story, because newspapers had been writing all about during months, and go home in tears. If those people had not been ignorant, they would have jailed all insolvent bankers, and have started a national investigation.

By 1913 the American people were so fed up with the continuous recessions, that they would believe any story the bankers would tell them, if it only served to stop those recessions. That is what the secretive 1910 Jekyll Island meeting[6] intended: To trick Woodrow Wilson into the worst American Suicide Act one can ever think of. By means of the 1913 Act of the Federal Reserve System, Congress officially gave full power to very few private bankers to determine the governmental monetary policy.[7]

---

6   see section 3.2 for the attendees

7   A decade ago, the very opposite happened in Iceland. Icelanders decided to take a financial blow, but not without putting all highest banking personnel into prison for a long time. Iceland's financial problems were over within a year.

An innocent pea picker in California in 1936
suffering a slow hunger death with her children[8]
For the rotten bankers these people were mere
disposables.

Mainly because he had himself fooled into agreeing with the Federal Reserve Act of 1913, which established the Federal Reserve System (FRS or FED). Note that the FRS is not a bank, nor is it federal (but privately owned), nor a semi-government institution (like a Central Bank). In democratic countries with a Central Bank, the latter is usually left alone, in order to have it decide its own policy, independently of the government. However, the Bank

---

8   Do not weep, my dear reader. These four innocents are in Heaven. Not those who made them suffer: and that, not because of some mysterious divine rejection, but because the perpetrators want neither nearness nor subjection to God.

president is elected by the government, usually from the political party with the highest number of votes. And yes, in cases of crisis, the government can overrule the decisions made by the President of the Central Bank.

2.2 Growth of the National Debt

The main problem in the US is obviously the ever increasing National Debt. Let us have a close look at the National Debt over Gross Domestic Product ratio.[9] The graph shows periods of debt accrual (dark grey areas below the ND/GDP curves) and of debt redemption in the subsequent years (light grey areas below the ND/GDP curves). From a fit of decreasing exponentials to the raw data (continuous lines through the discrete data points, starting in the year 1870), one concludes that, in periods free of wars and recessions, all debt was always redeemed within a period of 10 to 20 years. The essential anomaly is that, in order to fit the measured data, one needs to add an *increasing exponential*.

---

9   https://www.treasurydirect.gov
    See Appendix for a definition of terms

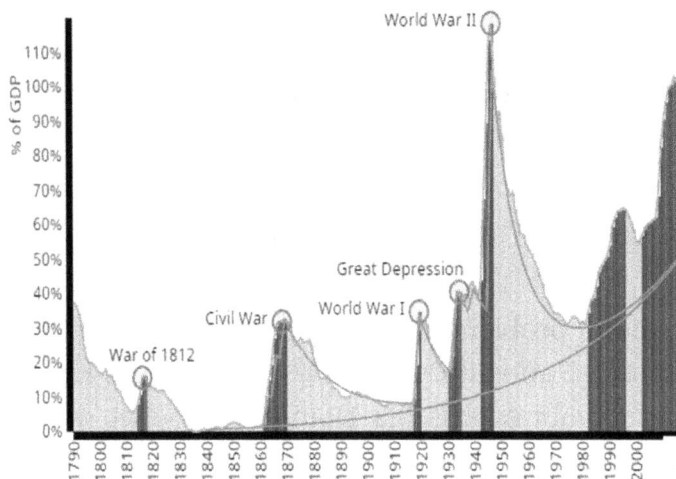

The discrete grey line starting in the year 1790 shows the "data" (the recorded national debt as a percentage of GDP). The smooth grey line, starting at the American Civil War, is the sum of the single exponentially increasing line, and a five decreasing exponentials. The latter have decay times of about 15 years, the recovery time of the American economy.

What does one observe in the above graph?

First, that the national debts incurred for the Civil War, World War I, and World War II, typically decay exponentially. This exponential decay reveals the strength of the American economy. The longer the tails are, the weaker the economy, and oppositely, the stronger the economy, the shorter the tails. One does not need to be an economist to understand this. One only needs to be an economist to have lost the ability to see the obvious, due to lamentable large-scale brainwashing.

The typical economic power displayed by the US economic recovery after a major catastrophe is about 15 years. Look up this number for whatever other country, and one understands why USA is the world-leading economic power.

Second observation. The rises of the two World War debts are nearly "instant" (that is, typically below 2 years) on the figure's time scale. The Civil War took longer, in agreement with the historical facts. Funny enough, the 2008 debt increase is not instant at all. How can this be, since the news of the House Market Bubble broke in 2006? The logical reaction would have been an instant explosion of the debt. What one sees instead, is that since 1980 the debt does all kind of things, apart from showing an instant increase.

Third observation. Even though the US economic power is about 15 years, a clearly visible increasing debt trend is visible. *What is worse, is that this underlying trend increases exponentially.* Clearly, something is actively making it impossible to the American economy to redeem that exponentially increasing debt. Anticipating on the next chapter, the exponentially increasing slope (lowest lying smooth grey line) is nothing but the *hidden* National Debt to the FED. That debt is hidden and not redeemable by the Federal Act of 1913, conceded to the banking mafia by President Woodrow Wilson.

Quite generally, in a civil war, one part of the country fights another part. Both parties must be heavily financed, because without money one can fight no war. That creates debt, both to domestic and foreign bankers, and for both contestants of the civil war. In a national war, the country as a whole fights a war with foreign countries. This creates debt, too, but with the advantage that there is but a single contestant.

A recession is nothing but an ordinary civil war, though not of Southerner Separationists against Northerner Unionists, *but of very few extremely immoral private bankers against the mostly ignorant and poor people.* This creates debt, too: the government has to borrow from those private banks to make a living possible for its people. It is easy to see that the people pay, and the banks own their mortgages.

However, in "100% democratic" USA, the privately run FED has full legal power to dictate

(i)   the amount of M3 money[10] in circulation;
(ii)   inflation;
(iii)   the monetary policy;
(iv)   the usurping interest rates required on loans to the government;
(v)   the Internal Revenue Service (IRS) collects taxes from all visible taxpayers, but the equally visible raised taxes do not end up in the national treasury, but in the dark FED, whose operations nobody knows.

---

10   See Appendix for a definition

2.3 M3 Money Supply Since 2007

The graphic below shows the year per year monthly percentile variations of the M_1, M_2, and M_3 money supplies.

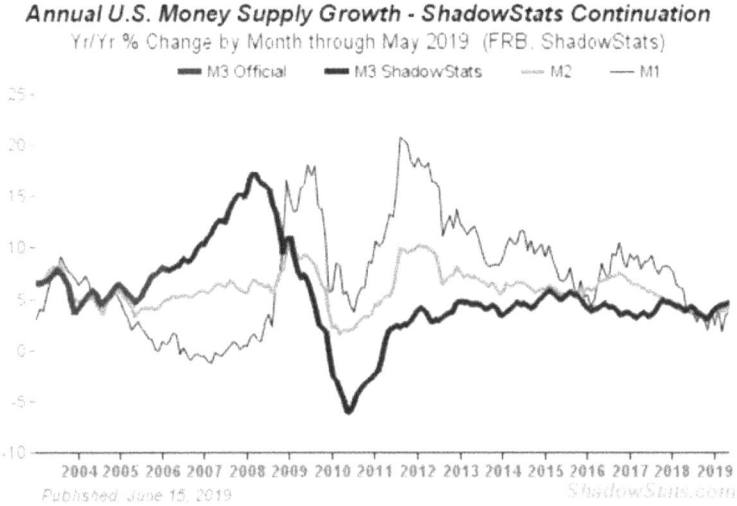

Annual U.S. Money Supply Growth - ShadowStats Continuation
Yr/Yr % Change by Month through May 2019 (FRB, ShadowStats)

The official M3 data stop in the year 2006. Why would the government withhold these figures from publicity? The only thing that comes to my mind is a direct FED intervention: The government does not give reason for hiding data of public concern. But why would one immediately suspect the FED? Because there is nobody else with that power, not even the very President! Of course it is not even possible, but obvious that whatever President has to hide something, but when known, that would have led to an avalanche of criticism. What did the press report about the author of that decision in 2007? nothing worthwhile to mention, given its impact.

2.4 Economic "Nobel Prizes" are Visibly Manipulated

The *Sveriges Riksbank Prize in Economic Sciences* "in Memory of Alfred Nobel", informally called the Nobel Prize in Economics, is a prize awarded each year for outstanding contributions in the field of economics. The prize was not one of the original awards set out in the will of Alfred Nobel. The winners of the prize receive their diploma and gold medal from the Swedish monarch at the same December 10 ceremony in Stockholm, as the Nobel laureates in physics, chemistry, physiology or medicine, and literature. The amount of money awarded to the economics laureates is also equal to that of the other prizes.

Below follow the tables summarizing all awards since 1969, the first year that the *Sveriges Riksbank* awarded the prize.

The awards are biased for several reasons. I do respect the American contribution to science and culture a lot, as should be obvious from everything I published to date; but I see no single reason why half the number of awardees should house in but a few American universities, with an overt overrepresentation of both Scandinavians and people of Jewish origin. This means that either the *Sveriges Riksbank* Prize Committee is biased, or economy is a country-specific discipline with no claim to universality. The former case is easy to solve. Simply leave the candidate election to the ten highest-ranked economists,[11] instead of to the Swedish Royal Bank, whose Nobel commission apparently has no clue about economic research.

Year	Awardee(s)	Matter
1969	Frisch, Tinbergen	dynamic models
1970	Samuelson	dynamic models
1971	Simon Kuznets	growth
1972	Hicks, Arrow	equilibrium theory
1973	Leontief	input-output method
1974	Myrdal, Hayek	money and fluctuations
1975	Kantorovich, Koopmans	optimum allocation of resources
1976	Friedman	stabilization policies
1977	Ohlin, Meade	capital movements
1978	Simon	decision-making
1979	Schultz, Lewis	developing countries

The second case is even simpler. If economy has no universal validity claim, it is by definition not a scientific discipline. Economy Prizes apparently have the scientific

---

11 No special sessions, no public insight into personal voting, and previous requirement of moral plight of withdrawal of the complete election team in case of a single threat to a single member

status of Peace Prizes: People with big promises and little achievements.

Year	Awardee(s)	Matter
1980	Klein	economic fluctuations
1981	Tobin	financial markets
1982	Stigler	market regulation
1983	Debreu	general equilibrium
1984	Stone	national accounts
1985	Modigliani	financial markets
1986	Buchanan	decision-making
1987	Solow	growth
1988	Allais	utilization of resources
1989	Haavelmo	econometrics

A second bias is apparent from the fact that only one woman figures among the awardees (hopefully, the reader is able to identify a few more).[12]

---

12 EZ treats women like Jews in the time of Moses: from his two God-given law tables (these form the only true Qur'an on this planet), particularly the tenth article, it is obvious that women are listed among men's properties: "You must not be envious of your neighbor's goods. You shall not be envious of his house nor his wife, nor anything that belongs to your neighbor." Moreover, in Jesus' time women were not considered authoritative witnesses while men were, by law. In case of adultery, the woman had to be stoned to death (not in practice but according to the law) yet the man went free. Summarizing, in the ancient Jewish society, like

Year	Awardee(s)	Matter
1990	Markowitz, Miller, Sharpe	financial economics
1991	Coase	property rights
1992	Becker	human nonmarket behavior
1993	Fogel, North	history of institutional change
1994	Harsanyi, Nash, Selten	non-cooperative game theory
1995	Lucas	rational expectations
1996	Mirrlees, Vickrey	incentives under asymmetric information
1997	Merton, Scholes	derivatives
1998	Sen	welfare economics
1999	Mundell	optimum currency

A third bias, specific for the matter column, is that not a single analysis of the role of the American Federal Reserve System appears, even though the FED is a planetary uniqueness: a private institute that has the exclusive and totally autonomous[13] right of daily determining the amount of M3 money supply, apparently at

---

in all ancient cultures, women were considered as mere property, and were expected to behave like that.

13 in the sense that neither president, nor government, not parliament have any say in it

liberty to hide these numbers from the government.

Year	Awardee(s)	Matter
2000	Heckman McFadden	selective samples discrete choice
2001	Akerlof, Spence, Stiglitz	asymmetric information
2002	Kahneman Smith	human decisions market mechanisms
2003	Engle, Granger	economic time series
2004	Kydland, Prescott	dynamic macroeconomics
2005	Aumann, Schelling	game theory applications in economy
2006	Phelps	intertemporal tradeoffs
2007	Hurwicz, Maskin, Myerson	mechanism design theory
2008	Paul Krugman	trade patterns
2009	Ostrom (♀), Williamson	economic governance

Year	Awardee(s)	Matter
2010	Diamond	search frictions
2011	Sargent	cause and effect
2012	Roth	market design
2013	Hansen, Fama, Shiller	empirical analysis of asset prices
2014	Tirole	market regulation
2015	Deaton	consumption
2016	Hart	contract theory
2017	Thaler	behavioral economics
2018	Romer, Nordhaus	climate change technological innovations

In whatever case, economy is a free science which ended up in the claws of a banking mafia. So are climate change, evolution theory, gender theory, biological species theory, and so forth. Every academic discipline that slightly touches upon politically correct issues, immediately turns into a FED-dominated field. This means the immediate death of the scientific discipline. It is really funny to notice that the 2018 reward for economy went to the topic of "climate change". Probably, someone forgot to mention that economy is not only linked to climate, but to entertainment industry and mortgage packages as well. To say the least...

2.5 Four US President Assassinations by Rothschild's Banking Mafia

The following article is written by Politicalvelcraft and Rense, and dates from November 2013.[14]

Case Closed:

JFK Killed After Shutting Down Rothschild's Federal Reserve

On June 4, 1963, a virtually unknown Presidential decree, Executive Order 11110, was signed with the authority to basically strip the Rothschild Bank of its power to loan money to the United States Federal Government at interest.

With the stroke of a pen, President Kennedy declared that the privately owned Rothschild Federal Reserve Bank would soon be out of business. The Christian Law Fellowship has exhaustively researched this matter through the Federal Register and Library of Congress.

We can now safely conclude that this

---

14 http://humansarefree.com/2013/11/
    jfk-killed-after-shutting-down.html

Executive Order has never been repealed, amended, or superseded by any subsequent Executive Order. In simple terms, it is still valid.

When President John Fitzgerald Kennedy signed this Order, it returned to the United States federal government, specifically the Treasury Department, the Constitutional power to create and issue currency - money – without going through the privately owned Rothschild Federal Reserve Bank.

President John Fitzgerald Kennedy
True Martyr for the sake of the US citizens

The Federal Reserve

A myth that all Americans live with is the charade known as the "Federal Reserve." It comes as a shock to many to discover that it is not an agency of the United States Government.

The name "Federal Reserve Bank" was designed to deceive, and it still does. It is not federal, nor is it owned by the government. It is privately owned.

It pays its own postage like any other corporation. Its employees are not in civil service. Its physical property is held under private deeds, and is subject to local taxation. Government property, as you know, is not.

It is an engine that has created private wealth that is unimaginable, even to the most financially sophisticated.

It has enabled an imperial elite to manipulate our economy for its own agenda and enlisted the government itself as its enforcer. It controls the times, dictates business, affects our homes and practically everything in which we are interested.

It takes powerful force to maintain an empire, and this one is no different. The concerns of the leadership of the "Federal Reserve" and its secretive international benefactors appear to go well beyond currency and interest rates.

Executive Order 11,110

President Kennedy's Executive Order 11,110 gave the Treasury Department the explicit authority:

"to issue silver certificates against any silver bullion, silver, or standard silver dollars in the Treasury."

This means that for every ounce of silver in the U.S. Treasury's vault, the government could introduce new money into circulation based on the silver bullion physically held there.

As a result, more than $4 billion in United States Notes were brought into circulation in $2 and $5 denominations.

$10 and $20 United States Notes were never circulated but were being printed by the Treasury Department when Kennedy was assassinated. It appears obvious that President Kennedy knew the Federal Reserve Notes being used as the purported legal currency were contrary to the Constitution of the United States of America. "United States Notes" were issued as an interest-free and debt-free currency backed by silver reserves in the U.S. Treasury.

Jacob Rothschild

We compared a "Federal Reserve Note" issued

from the private central bank of the United States (the Federal Reserve Bank a.k.a. Federal Reserve System), with a "United States Note" from the U.S. Treasury issued by President Kennedy's Executive Order.

They almost look alike, except one says "Federal Reserve Note" on the top while the other says "United States Note". Also, the Federal Reserve Note has a green seal and serial number while the United States Note has a red seal and serial number.

President Kennedy was assassinated on November 22, 1963 and the United States Notes he had issued were immediately taken out of circulation. Federal Reserve Notes continued to serve as the legal currency of the nation.

According to the United States Secret Service, 99% of all U.S. paper "currency" circulating in 1999 are Federal Reserve Notes.

Kennedy knew that if the silver-backed United States Notes were widely circulated, they would have eliminated the demand for Federal Reserve Notes. This is a very simple matter of economics. The USN was backed by silver and the FRN was not backed by anything of intrinsic value.

Executive Order 11110 should have prevented the national debt from reaching its current level (virtually all of the nearly $9 trillion in federal debt has been created since 1963) if LBJ or any subsequent President were to enforce it.

It would have almost immediately given the U.S. Government the ability to repay its debt without going to the private Federal Reserve Banks and being charged interest to create new "money".

Executive Order 11,110 gave the U.S.A. the ability to, once again, create its own money backed by silver and realm value worth something.

Again, according to our own research, just five months after Kennedy was assassinated, no more of the Series 1958 "Silver Certificates" were issued either, and they were subsequently removed from circulation.

Perhaps the assassination of JFK was a warning to all future presidents not to interfere with the private Rothschild Federal Reserve's control over the creation of money.

It seems very apparent that President Kennedy challenged the "**powers that exist behind U.S. and world finance**".

On November 22, 1963, JFK was shot dead in Dallas, Texas, in extremely strange circumstances. Phyllis Hall, a nurse who was part of desperate attempts to save the life of President John F Kennedy after he was assassinated has claimed he was shot by a "mystery bullet."

There is also strong evidence involving Lyndon B. Johnson (The following USA President) in the assassination conspiracy.

Below follows the story of three earlier US Presidents murdered by the Rothschild banking cartel.

Abraham Lincoln

Abraham Lincoln worked valiantly to prevent the Rothschild's attempts to involve themselves in financing the Civil War.

Interestingly, it was the Czar of Russia who provided the needed assistance against the British and French, who were among the driving forces behind the secession of the South and her subsequent financing.

Russia intervened by providing naval forces for the Union blockade of the South in European waters, and by letting both countries know that if they attempted to join the Confederacy with military forces, they would also have to go to war with Russia.

The Rothschild interests did succeed, through their agent Treasury Secretary Salmon P. Chase, to force a bill (the National Banking Act) through Congress creating a federally chartered central bank that had the power to issue U.S. Bank Notes.

Afterward, Lincoln warned the American people:

"The money power preys upon the nation in time of peace and conspires against it in times of adversity. It is more despotic than monarchy, more insolent than autocracy, more selfish than bureaucracy. I see in the near future a crisis approaching that unnerves me, and causes me to tremble for the safety of our country. Corporations have been enthroned, an era of corruption will follow, and the money power of the country will endeavor to prolong its reign by working upon the prejudices of the people, until the wealth is aggregated in a few hands, and the republic is destroyed."

Lincoln continued to fight against the central bank, and some now believe that it was his anticipated success in influencing Congress to limit the life of the Bank of the United States to just the war years that was the motivating factor behind his assassination.

The Lone Assassin Myth is Born

Modern researchers have uncovered evidence of a massive conspiracy that links the following parties to the Bank of Rothschild: Lincoln's Secretary of War Edwin Stanton, John Wilkes Booth, his eight co-conspirators, and over seventy government officials and businessmen involved in the conspiracy.

When Booth's diary was recovered by Stanton's troops, it was delivered to Stanton. When it was later produced during the investigation, eighteen pages had been ripped out.

These pages, containing the aforementioned names, were later found in the attic of one of Stanton's descendants.

From Booth's trunk, a coded message was found that linked him directly to Judah P. Benjamin, the Civil War campaign manager in the South for the House of Rothschild. When the war ended, the key to the code was found in Benjamin's possession.

The assassin, portrayed as a crazed lone gunman with a few radical friends, escaped by way of the only bridge in Washington not guarded by Stanton's troops.

"Booth" was located hiding in a barn near Port Royal, Virginia, three days after escaping from Washington. He was shot by a soldier named Boston Corbett, who fired without orders.

Whether or not the man killed was Booth is

still a matter of contention, but the fact remains that whoever it was, he had no chance to identify himself.

It was Secretary of War Edwin Stanton who made the final identification. Some now believe that a dupe was used and that the real John Wilkes Booth escaped with Stanton's assistance.

Mary Todd Lincoln, upon hearing of her husband's death, began screaming, "Oh, that dreadful house!" Earlier historians felt that this spontaneous utterance referred to the White House.

Some now believe it may have been directed to Thomas W. House, a gun runner, financier, and agent of the Rothschild's during the Civil War, who was linked to the anti-Lincoln, pro-banker interests.

Andrew Jackson

Andrew Jackson was the first President from west of the Appalachians. He was unique for the times in being elected by the voters, without the direct support of a recognized political organization.

He vetoed the renewal of the charter for the Bank of the United States on July 10, 1832.

In 1835, President Andrew Jackson declared his disdain for the international bankers:

"You are a den of vipers. I intend to rout you out, and by the Eternal God I will rout you out. If the people only understood the rank injustice of our money and banking system, there would be a revolution before morning."

There followed an (unsuccessful) assassination attempt on President Jackson's life. Jackson had

told his vice president, Martin Van Buren,
    "The bank, Mr. Van Buren, is trying to kill me."
Was this the beginning of a pattern of intrigue that would plague the White House itself over the coming decades? Was his (and Lincoln's) death related by an invisible thread to the international bankers?

James Garfield

President James Abram Garfield, our 20th President, had previously been Chairman of the House Committee on Appropriations and was an expert on fiscal matters.

Upon his election, among other things, he

appointed an unpopular collector of customs at New York, whereupon the two Senators from New York - Roscoe Conkling and Thomas Platt - resigned their seats.

President Garfield openly declared that whoever controls the supply of currency would control the business and activities of all the people.

After only four months in office, President Garfield was shot at a railroad station on July 2, 1881. Another coincidence.

The Trail of Blood Continues

In the 70's and 80's, Congressman Larry P. McDonald spearheaded efforts to expose the hidden holdings and intentions of the international money interests.

His efforts ended on August 31, 1983, when he was killed when Korean Airlines 007 was "accidentally" shot down in Soviet airspace. A strange coincidence, it would seem.

Senator John Heinz and former Senator John Tower had served on powerful Senate banking and finance committees and were outspoken critics of the Federal Reserve and the Eastern Establishment.

On April 4, 1991, Senator John Heinz was killed in a plane crash near Philadelphia. On the next day, April 5, 1991, former Senator John Tower was also killed in a plane crash. The coincidences seem to mount.

Attempts to just audit the Federal Reserve continue to meet with failure. It is virtually impossible to muster support for any issue that has the benefit of a media blackout.

Beginning of a Series

For many years, numerous authors have attempted to sound the alarm that there exists a hidden "shadow government" that actually rules America.

Most of us have dismissed these "conspiracy theory" views as extremist and unrealistic. However, when I had the opportunity to have lunch with Otto von Habsburg, member of the European Parliament, he made two remarks that caught my attention.

The first was: **"The ignorance in America is overwhelming."** Indeed, the contrast in general awareness of world affairs between the average American and the average European is striking.

It was his second observation that really provoked me: **"The concentration of power in America is frightening."**

As a reasonably circumspect senior executive, having spent three decades in international finance and viewing America as a broadly based representative democracy, his remark shocked me. It prompted me to do some more homework. The results of my inquiries are most disturbing.

References

James W. Wardner, "The Planned Destruction of America"

Craig Roberts, "Kill Zone: A Sniper Looks at Dealey Plaza;"

Ron Paul, "The Ron Paul Survival Report" (a newsletter by a former congressman on monetary issues, personal survival, etc.)

2.6 Currency Groups

From time-dependent currency data over the years 1970-2018, made available by Prof. Werner Antweiler,[15] I calculated the below 2D map. The distance between currency hexagons is proportional to their correlation function, which increases to unity when two currencies vary equally in time, apart from a constant multiplication factor. The correlation function vanishes when two currencies fluctuate independently from one another. The correlation can sink to negative unity when they show a perfect anti-correlation, meaning that when one increases, the other decreases proportionally.

The below 2D graph must be interpreted as rolled up along the page width, such that the twice represented USD reduces to a single surface of a 3D cylinder. The circumference of the 3D cylinder is equal to the height of the graph (slightly below 7").

The country-specific currency labels (like CNY for the Chinese Yuan, or RUB for the Russian Ruble) can be found on every financial website.

Two hexagons contain two currencies (Italy & Spain, and Germany & Austria), as they had a correlation coefficient above 99%.

---

15 © 2019, University of British Columbia. His own sources: are IMF, World Bank, and OECD. Only the Chinese and Russian currencies I found on the web myself. Too bad their temporal ranges were smaller than the Antweiler data.

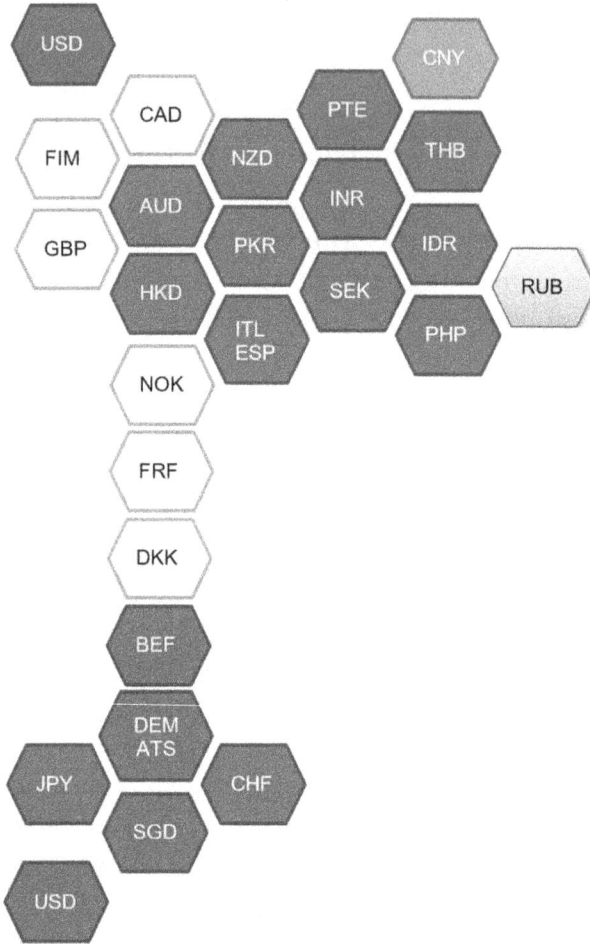

***The perfect currency signature of a hijacked
economy.*** *The USD operates totally independent of all
other currencies. Apparently, the interests of those
determining the USD currency exchange rate have an
agenda, which strives at a goal quite different from the
American citizens' common good.*

CHAPTER 3
What the FED really is

3.1 Simple Approach

There is one enormous inconsistency in what the FED says about itself. On one hand, it says that the FED is a unique government-**in**dependent institute that "channels all of its profits to the Treasury Department of the government", less the 6% dividend mentioned in Chapter 3, while on the other, the US national debt skyrockets like nowhere else on the planet, as do the total assets of the 12 Federal Reserve Banks. Hence the US has the unique property on our planet, that its National Treasury is complemented by the FED, whose assets skyrocket in about the same amount as the US national debt. We will first take a simplified view:

- Do the US produce useless, unsellable products? No.
- Do the US sell much less abroad than buy from abroad? No.
- Is US technology retrograde? No.
- Are Americans lazy? No.
- Does the US budget look like that of a socialist-welfare European country? No.[16]
- Are Americans dumber than Europeans? No.
- Do the US spend more on military? Yes.

According to this list of facts, the US deficit is entirely due to its military expenses. These somehow *must* end up in the FED's pockets, else the total assets of the FED would not skyrocket, but slowly and steadily increase due to the yearly deficit. As a matter of fact, all military expenses are but a mere burden for the American people, as the only thing the American people get in return for those expenses, are coffins of their sons and daughters. Since moreover, the FED supplies M3 money to the USD market on its own authority (i.e., independent of government),[17]

---

16 The US spends much less on both social issues (pensions, unemployment salaries, care, education) and its own bureaucracy than European socialist countries do.

17 To print new currency "ex novo" differs day-night from *recycling* currency. In the latter case, the amount of newly printed currency exactly equals the amount of destroyed old currency, while in the former, nothing is destroyed, However, "ex novo" currency

it should somehow be included in or at least juxtaposed to the US yearly budget.

3.2 The Humanitarian Hoax

The Humanitarian Hoax[18] is a deliberate and deceitful tactic of presenting a destructive policy as altruistic. The humanitarian huckster presents himself as a compassionate advocate when in fact he is the disguised enemy.

Most Americans do not realize that the Federal Reserve is NOT constitutionally part of the United States Government and is not even a bank! The Federal Reserve is a system. International banker Marilyn Barnewall explains that the Federal Reserve System is a privately held corporation owned by bankers and it is most definitely not part of the federal government.

The Federal Reserve Act that created the Federal Reserve System (Fed) was passed in Congress on

---

printing is nothing but a hidden tax, by devaluating the value of the citizen's dollars.. In the case of the FED, which is a private institution, the currency devaluation is exactly the same. . What differs, is the Treasury's debt. More about that in the next chapter.

18 https://canadafreepress.com/article/the-humanitarian-hoax-of-the-federal-reserve-system, by Linda Goudsmit, April 24, 2018

December 22, 1913 and signed into law by President
Woodrow Wilson the next day. Barnewall describes the
dramatic effects of its passage.

> The Act transferred the right to print currency from
> the United States Congress to an independent and
> privately-owned entity calling itself a bank but which
> is not a bank and changing the Constitution which
> cannot be changed without Amending it. The Fed is
> somewhat federal in form, but is very privately owned
> and operated. President Wilson lived to regret signing
> The Federal Reserve Act and on his death bed is
> quoted as saying:
>
> "I am a most unhappy man. I have unwittingly
> ruined my country. A great industrial nation is
> controlled by its system of credit. Our system of
> credit is concentrated. The growth of the nation,
> therefore, and all our activities are in the hands of a
> few men."

So, who are these men and why was President Wilson so
remorseful about signing the Federal Reserve Act? And
why is the Federal Reserve System so disingenuously
named that the average citizen assumes it is a banking
institution and part of the federal government?

Sometimes it is necessary to look back to understand
the present and anticipate the future.

Banking in the world has a long history that began
with merchant trading. People living in small isolated
agricultural communities exchanged pigs for goats or

wheat for milk and personal bartering among members of the community was enough to satisfy their survival needs - there was no need for currency or banking. As populations grew and trade between communities began, currency was introduced to make commerce more efficient. Currency was assigned a monetary value and buying and selling with money replaced bartering as the preferred form of commerce.

Determining the value of currency and the relative value of the goats, pigs, wheat, and milk being bought and sold was the beginning of banking. Currency use requires that people trust the banknotes and coins to represent an actual and real valued commodity. Gold was chosen as the standard that backed the currency and banks became repositories for both. Today we use fiat currency - money - as the medium of exchange and it is the taxpayers' labor that backs it. WHAT?

Think about it. As long as the Federal government can tax its citizen labor force and confiscate their money to pay its debts it is the taxpayers who are actually backing the currency. We the people are the 21st century gold standard!

Banking is and always has been a for-profit business. The Federal Reserve Bank is no exception.

Prior to 1913 there were two central banks in the United States - both non-governmental entities. The First Bank of the United States (1791-1811) was chartered by the First Congress in 1790 and modeled after the Bank of England. Thomas Jefferson opposed the First Bank as an engine for speculation, financial manipulation, and corruption. When its 20-year charter expired it was not renewed.

Its successor bank, the Second Bank of the United States (1816-1836) was also a private bank with public duties and Andrew Jackson, like Thomas Jefferson, opposed the Second Bank as an engine of corruption. Jackson, who became president in 1828, was unable to get the bank dissolved but refused to renew its charter. President Jackson required all Federal land payments be made in gold or silver which produced the Panic of 1837. Runs on the banks, bank failures, and economic depression followed. The panic unleashed riots and domestic unrest which ultimately resulted in more state policing and more professional police forces.

The depression lasted five years until 1842 when the American economy began to rebound. In 1848 the California gold rush boosted the economy and by 1850 the US economy was booming again. Still, a national system was required to facilitate banking between regions that could avert another financial crisis. When President Woodrow Wilson signed the 1913 Federal Reserve Act the current central banking system of the United States was created. 12 United States cities were chosen as locations for one of 12 Federal Reserve District Banks. This is how it happened.

A secret gathering took place on Jekyll Island November 1910 that laid the foundation for the Federal Reserve System in the United States. In attendance were:

Senator Nelson W. Aldrich, chairman of the US Senate Finance Committee, chair of the National Monetary Commission

Abram Piatt Andrew, assistant secretary of the US Treasury and special assistant to the National Monetary commission

Charles D. Norton, president of the Morgan dominated First National Bank of New York

Frank Vanderlip, president of National City Bank

Henry P. Davison, senior partner at J.P. Morgan & Co.

Benjamin Strong, representing J.P. Morgan

Paul Warburg partner at Kuhn, Loeb & Co.

The clandestine 1910 Jekyll Island meeting produced draft legislation for the creation of the U.S. central bank and the Aldrich Plan was incorporated into the 1913 Federal Reserve Act. Why is the Jekyll Island history so important? Why was the meeting so clandestine? Because the secret meeting at Jekyll Island failed to disclose its connections to the Bank of England.

J.P. Morgan & Co., and Kuhn, Loeb & Co. are the New York representatives of the Rothschilds Bank of England which means that the American Federal Reserve system is under the control of the Bank of England. The howling anti-Semitic memes that Jews control the banking is deliberate and misleading. The Federal Reserve Cartel, the Rothschild (Jewish), Rockefeller (Baptist), and Morgan (Episcopalian) families, are globalist, multi-religious, and non-denominational. This is how it works.

The Humanitarian Hoax of the Federal Reserve System is evident in its deliberately deceptive name. There is an enormous public misconception that the Federal Reserve System exists to protect and to serve America. It doesn't. The FED is a for-profit corporation of globalist world bankers seeking to internationalize the world for their own power and profit. The FED is NOT an advocate of American sovereignty or America-first policies. The FED is not altruistic - it is a hoax.

President Donald Trump is an American patriot committed to American sovereignty and is, therefore, an existential enemy of the FED.

The globalist elite use our Federal Reserve System to manipulate world economies through their banking malfeasance. By raising interest rates, lowering interest rates, and printing money they control the availability of funds to their member banks that make loans to individuals and businesses. World banking is based on the US dollar, so FED decisions in America affect inflation, employment, and production worldwide.

When the FED raises interest rates in America the interest rates go up on consumer credit cards, car loans, and mortgages making it harder for American consumers to get credit. This causes the US economy to shrink in the private sector. Raising interest rates makes business loans more expensive, increases unemployment, and degrades productivity which shrinks the US economy in the business sector. Most threatening is that raising interest rates increases the US national debt and makes it increasingly difficult to service the debt and repay the loans.

Conversely, the FED can lower interest rates which floods the market with cheap money to artificially stimulate the economy - raising and lowering interest rates both have political consequences.

The power of the Federal Reserve System to collapse the American economy is held by a private corporation of international globalist bankers whose long-range political goals are to internationalize the world and establish a New World Order of one-government ruled by themselves of course. Individuals who cannot repay their debts go bankrupt - so do countries.

The existential threat to American sovereignty is Globalism. Globalism's one-world government with one bank, one police force, one army, one flag, one language, one educational curriculum, one currency, one world with one ruling class - the globalist elite. Make no mistake - globalism is a catastrophic return to a master/slave feudal infrastructure.

Globalism is a non-denominational power grab by the globalist elite using anti-Semitism as a strategic sideshow. Sideshows are diverting incidents or issues designed to distract attention away from bigger issues. The FED is manipulating the world economies while its globalist armies have boots on the ground indoctrinating America to accept collectivism and one-world government via the mainstream media, the educational system, Obama's Resistance movement, and an unremitting assault on American traditional values.

If the Humanitarian Hoax of the Federal Reserve System continues, our Republic and the Constitutional freedoms our forefathers created will cease to exist. The globalist New World Order will be imposed by the ruling class of globalist elite. The useful idiots who support the globalist elite power grab, including the anti-Semitic memes that reinforce it, will succeed in killing America.

The globalist soldiers are the same useful idiots marching toward slavery in Goethe's famous quote:

"None are more hopelessly enslaved than those who falsely believe they are free as they are marched into servitude."

Goethe articulates President Woodrow Wilson's remorse.

3.3 The 2008 Depression

An excellent documentary describing many details of the housing market depression, initiated in the USA in 2007, is "The Big Short", which is based on the homonym book by Michael Lewis. From the movie's Wikipedia site I quote the plot:[19]

The film consists of three separate but concurrent stories, loosely connected by their actions in the years leading up to the 2007 housing market crash.

In 2005, eccentric hedge fund manager Michael Burry (Christian Bale) discovers that the United States housing market, based on high-risk subprime loans, is extremely unstable. Anticipating the market's collapse in the second quarter of 2007, as interest rates would rise from adjustable-rate mortgages, he proposes to create a credit default swap market, allowing him to bet against market-based mortgage-backed securities, for profit.

His long-term bet, exceeding $1 billion, is accepted by major investment and commercial banks, but as it requires paying substantial monthly premiums, it sparks his clients' vocal unhappiness, believing he is "wasting" capital. Many demand that he

---

19   https://en.wikipedia.org/wiki/The_Big_Short_(film)

reverse and sell, but Burry refuses. Under pressure, he eventually restricts withdrawals, angering investors. Eventually, the market collapses and his fund's value increases by 489% with an overall profit of over $2.69 billion.

Deutsche Bank salesman Jared Vennett (based on Greg Lippmann, played by Ryan Gosling), the executive in charge of global asset-backed securities trading at Deutsche Bank, is one of the first to understand Burry's analysis, learning from one of the bankers who sold Burry an early credit default swap. Using his quant to verify that Burry is likely correct, he decides to enter the market, earning a fee on selling the swaps to firms who will profit when the underlying bonds fail. A misplaced phone call alerts FrontPoint hedge fund manager Mark Baum (based on Steve Eisman, played by Steve Carell), who is motivated to buy swaps from Vennett due to his low regard for banks' ethics and business models. Vennett explains that the packaging of subprime loans into collateralized debt obligations (CDOs) rated at AAA ratings will guarantee their eventual collapse.

Conducting a field investigation in South Florida, the FrontPoint team discovers that mortgage brokers are profiting by selling their mortgage deals to Wall Street banks, who pay higher margins for the riskier mortgages, creating the bubble, prompting them to buy swaps from Vennett. In early 2007, as these loans begin to default, CDO prices somehow rise and ratings agencies refuse to downgrade the bond ratings. Baum discovers conflicts of interest and dishonesty amongst the credit rating agencies from an acquaintance at Standard & Poor's. Baum's employees question Vennett's motives, yet he maintains his position and invites Baum and company to the American Securitization Forum in Las Vegas. Interviewed by Baum, CDO manager Wing Chau, on behalf of an investment bank, describes how synthetic CDOs create chains of increasingly large bets on faulty loans – up to 20 times as much money as the loans themselves. A horrified Baum realizes that the fraud will completely collapse the global economy. He purchases as much as possible, profiting at the banks' expense and waits until the last minute to sell. Baum's fund makes a profit of $1 billion, and he laments that the banks won't accept blame for the crisis and that people will scapegoat immigrants, teachers and the poor.

Young investors Charlie Geller and Jamie Shipley accidentally discover a prospectus by Vennett, convincing them to invest in swaps, as it fits their strategy of buying cheap insurance with big potential payouts. Below the capital threshold for an ISDA Master Agreement required to enter into trades like Burry's and Baum's, they enlist the aid of retired securities trader Ben Rickert. When the bond values and CDOs rise despite defaults, Geller suspects the banks of committing fraud. The trio also visit the Forum, learning that the U.S. Securities and Exchange Commission has no regulations to monitor mortgage-backed security activity. They successfully make even more profit than other hedge funds by shorting the higher-rated AA mortgage securities, as they were considered highly stable and carried a much higher payout ratio.

Geller and Shipley are initially ecstatic, but Rickert is disgusted, citing the impending collapse and its effects; **when unemployment goes up 1%, 40,000 people will die.** Furthermore, they realize the banks and the ratings agency are maintaining the value of their CDOs in order to sell and short them before the inevitable crash. Horrified, they try to tip off the press and their families about the upcoming disaster and the rampant fraud but nobody believes them. As the market starts collapsing, Ben, on vacation in England, sells their swaps. Ultimately, they make a profit of $80 million, with their faith in the system broken.

Jared Vennett makes $47 million in commissions selling off the swaps. Mark Baum becomes more gracious from the financial fallout, and his staff continues to operate their fund. Charlie Geller and Jamie Shipley go their separate ways after unsuccessfully trying to sue the ratings agencies, with Charlie moving to Charlotte to start a family, and Jamie still running the fund. Ben Rickert returns to his peaceful retirement. Michael Burry closes his fund after public backlash and multiple IRS audits, now only investing in water securities. The banks responsible for the crisis escape any consequences for their actions. It is noted that as of 2015, banks are selling CDOs again under a new label: "Bespoke Tranche Opportunity".

Comparing McKay's movie plot to the book description, one can observe the movie storyline follows Lewis' book's quite closely:[20]

The Big Short describes several of the main players in the creation of the credit default swap market that sought to bet against the collateralized debt obligation (CDO) bubble and thus ended up profiting from the financial crisis of 2007–08. The book also highlights the eccentric nature of the type of person who bets against the market or goes against the grain. The work follows people who believed the bubble was going to burst, like Meredith Whitney, who predicted the demise of Citigroup and Bear Stearns; Steve Eisman, an outspoken hedge fund manager; Greg Lippmann, a Deutsche Bank trader; Eugene Xu, a quantitative analyst who created the first CDO market by matching buyers and sellers; the founders of Cornwall Capital, who started a hedge fund in their garage with $110,000 and built it into $120 million when the market crashed; and Michael Burry, an ex-neurologist who created Scion Capital.

The book also highlights some people involved in the biggest losses created by the market crash: like Merrill's $300 million mezzanine CDO manager Wing Chau; Howie Hubler, known as the person who lost $9 billion in one trade, the second largest single loss in

---

20 https://en.wikipedia.org/wiki/The_Big_Short

history; and Joseph Cassano's AIG Financial Products, which suffered over $99 billion in losses.

Reception

The book was shortlisted for the 2010 Financial Times and Goldman Sachs Business Book of the Year Award. It spent 28 weeks on The New York Times' non-fiction bestseller list. It also received the 2011 Robert F. Kennedy Center for Justice and Human Rights Book Award.

Until here the Wikipedia quotes.

Undoubtedly, they are extremely positive, both about Lewis' book, and about McKay's movie. They are praised abundantly by The New York Times and Washington Post, as well as by many survivor banks like Goldman Sachs. The survivor banks were those who invented the trash mortgage packages and CDO's in the first place. And as the movie claims, the survivor banks now continue selling BTO's, which are nothing but renamed CDO's.

Now what exactly is going on here? Something does not seem to fit. From my perspective, however, everything fits, and quite nicely so. Simply consider the banks overseen by the Federal Reserve System as a single banking mafia, with a single head. Obviously, he is in dire need to explain to the public why the FED missed such a financial bubble, which three independent individuals saw coming with two years of anticipation.

My first conclusion is that the FED knew of these people's movements all along. The FED guys are not *that* stupid. My second conclusion is that the FED-grouped banks were all instructed to short the mortgage packages as well, though in such a subtle way, that the three independent researchers did not notice. My third conclusion is that, while the researchers could not believe the bubble would not burst, even though all financial indicators were red hot (failures to pay the mortgages, exponential fraud increase), the FED-controlled banks were fraudulently keeping the mortgage package prizes high, in order to sell them to uninformed Eurasian banks. Once done with selling all their mortgage packages, they allowed the prices of those packages to crash. My fourth conclusion is that the researches only got tiny scraps of their profits, had the FED not played fraudulently. Upon summing up all American and Eurasian losses due to the American Housing Bubble, one does not even reach 1% of the profits made by the independent researchers. My fifth conclusion is that the remaining 99% of the gain ended up in eight of the nine FED-handled banks:[21]

---

21 Dr. Ken Matto, January 18, 2012. See, e.g., https://www.scionofzion.com/federalreserve.htm; https://forum.woodenboat.com/The-Bilge; https://www.onepoliticalplaza.com/t-13319-1.html; https://hotcopper.com.au/threads/the-federal-reserve-history-of-lies-thievery.1663181/

Rothschild Bank of London
Warburg Bank of Hamburg
Rothschild Bank of Berlin
Kuhn Loeb of New York
Lazard Brothers of Paris
Israel Moses Seif Banks of Italy
Goldman Sachs Bank of New York
Warburg Bank of Amsterdam
Chase Manhattan Bank of New York

Remember the final congress in McKay's movie, when Baum refutes the owner of Bear Bank, in a five minute talk? While Baum was talking, Bear's shares fell by 40%. Everybody left the room, eager to get rid of their Bear shares as soon as possible. Oops. I forgot the tiny detail: the next speaker planned was ex-FED president Alan Greenspan, who retired in favor of Ben Bernanke in January 31st, 2006, just a year ago. In the movie, the Baum-Bear audience was depicted too fixed on selling their Bear shares, to give any importance to the last talk of the session, that of Greenspan.

What exactly is the meaning of this filmic addition? It adds nothing to the plot, but a split-second zoom-in on Greenspan's disappointed face. It adds nothing to the storyline, either, as the FED has not been mentioned once in the full movie. What could possibly motivate McKay to insert a totally useless, humorless, impertinent scene to his masterpiece?

The answer is as simple as always. As Bernanke was likely to be held co-responsible for the 2008 exchange crash, he should better not be mentioned at all: From FED's perspective, the sooner the people forget about the FED, the better. So why introduce the FED, instead of silencing it completely?

This is nothing but the well-known subliminal technique often used in adds. *The audience sees the disappointed face of Greenspan long enough to infer that the FED had absolutely nothing to do with the 2008 global financial crisis.*

Exactly the same holds for Baum's interviewing the CDO manager Wing Chau, who describes how synthetic CDOs create chains of increasingly large bets on faulty loans – up to 20 times as much money as the loans themselves. Flash-backs of people betting on bets are shown. That is nonsensical, obviously. Nobody bets on a bet, when a direct bet is possible, too. It is but one more way to whitewash a hideous crime perpetrated by the FED.

EPILOGUE
Can One Fight This Monster?

The FED mafia is a master of deceit. Since they own the global mass media, the biggest movie companies (SONY, Hollywood), and nearly all the world's money, one might just as well sink into despair: Can the FED be fought at all? Of course. We humans can fight anything material, and exceptionally, something spiritual as well. The former category includes the FED. The latter category includes evil spirits, and they had better be left in the hands of Catholic priests.

Rothschild's baby, the all-devouring FED monster, can be *fought* indeed, but cannot be *defeated*. It will live as long as God allows it to. Standard question: well, how can an infinitely good God allow the existence of something evil? The philosophical answer is simple, although I doubt it will make any impression: God allows a lower evil only if a higher good results. Since I never had any special visions, I know as little of Divine Providence as my reader does.

But since Matthew 7:13-14,10 reads

"Enter by the narrow gate; for wide is the gate and broad is the way that leads to destruction, and there

are many who go in by it. Because narrow is the gate
and difficult is the way which leads to life, and there
are few who find it."

I suppose there is no other interpretation possible than
that most of us end up in hell. Well, **given** that these are
the Divine statistics, it is better to try hard in doing
something good down here. If we cannot kill the beast,
because it does not fit in with Divine Providence, we had
better die in the attempt.

APPENDIX 1

The Money Masters
by Patrick S.J. Carmack[22]

BASEL I

In 1988 a faceless, un-elected group of bankers met in Basel, Switzerland at the Bank for International Settlements ("BIS")[23] – the "Central Banker's bank"

---

22 http://www.themoneymasters.com/
23 The "investopedia website", under even tighter EZ-control than Wikipedia, mentions that a so-called "Basel Committee on Banking Supervision" was formed in 1974 by central bankers from the G10 countries, and headquartered in the offices of the Bank for International Settlements (BIS) in Basel, Switzerland. "The purpose of the accords is to ensure that financial institutions have enough capital on account to meet obligations and absorb unexpected losses." The website fails to mention (i) that these "central bankers" are individuals without government mandate, (ii) who these "central bankers" are or how and on basis of what personal qualities their election proceeds, and (iii) what extreme consequences these private agreements have for non-member countries, like causing a 26-year long depression in Japan. In the context of Basel II it defines "the three pillars" of a "clean" banking policy as being (i) minimum capital requirements, (ii) supervisory review of an institution's capital adequacy and

which even Swiss authorities may not enter – and in their "Basel I accords" agreed to a set of minimum capital requirements (8%) for banks. This was a number fine for some banks, but higher than what was in place for France and especially Japanese banks. To raise more capital to reach the 8% level, French and Japanese banks had to reduce loans, causing a recession in France and a depression in Japan, one from which Japan has never fully recovered.

BASEL II

In 2004, the same group met and agreed to Basel II ("The Return of Basel I")– which required banks to value their capital based on market values, or "mark-to-the-market." These rules were approved for the US on November 1, 2007. The declining housing market set off a chain reaction due in part to Basel II which banks knew was coming and constricted credit in anticipation of. The next month, December, 2007 the stock market collapsed and the Great Recession began in earnest.

---

internal assessment process, and (iii) effective use of disclosure as a lever to strengthen market discipline and encourage sound banking practices including supervisory review.

This should have been no surprise to the Japanese, nor to the BIS bankers. Full implementation of Basel II was subsequently delayed in the US until 2009. Basel II has been blamed for actually increasing the effect of the housing crisis as banks had to reduce lending to increase their capital as the value of mortgages they hold declined. This produced a downhill snowball effect on home prices and then on nearly everything else as lending and the economy contracted.

BASEL III

Not content with two massive regulatory failures, the same bankers have now produced Basel III ("The Revenge of Basel I & II"). Like Basel I & II, Basel III increases capital requirements yet again, in a series of steps beginning in 2013 with the start of the gradual phasing-in of the higher minimum capital requirements not completed until 2018. The BIS bankers have imposed this and are forcing their home governments to get in line, as has the UK, the US and most other developed nations. It is truly a global rule by central bankers acting in concert/cabal.

An OECD study estimates that the medium-term harmful impact of Basel III implementation on GDP growth is in the range of –0.05% to –0.15% per year – just what's needed in a worldwide recession! To meet the capital requirements effective in 2015 banks are estimated to need to increase their lending spreads on average by about 0.15%. The capital requirements effective as of 2019 could increase bank lending spreads by about 0.5%. Rising interest rates could significantly hurt small bank capital positions because a 3% upward swing in interest rates could drop a bank's capital by 30%, placing the bank in an undercapitalized position, forcing it dramatically to reduce loans. Again, the downhill snowball effect.

The proposed Basel III regulatory capital requirements are an immense and unnecessary burden that will actually threaten the existence of banks with under $1billion in assets. These new regulations will further drive consolidation into a few bigger banks. Some on Wall Street, like mergers and acquisitions expert John Slater, predict that Basel III's compliance costs will lead to a merger boom, and that in the next 3-5 years 20-30 percent of all banks will merge, further consolidating wealth in fewer and fewer hands. That is the object – world bank/economic and hence political control by a handful of un-elected, unaccountable, international bankers beholden to no one, many of whom have ethics only Machiavelli could admire and worldviews that most people on earth would consider abhorrent.

Advantages

Better Control/Reduction of Business Cycle Fluctuations (the Boom/Bust Cycles)

Elimination of Bank Runs

Dramatic Reduction of the National Debt (elimination when fully implemented)

Dramatic Reduction of Private Debt

National Output Gains of 10%

The IMF authors noted that all five benefits of the Plan were supported by their research. That is true. Caveat: however, absent safeguards the Chicago Plan per se would dangerously increase Leviathan's (the State) control over the economy (while reducing direct private bank control – a good thing in itself), and *it does not abolish fiat money* which would be even more subject to political control under the Chicago Plan. *As noted in the Monetary Reform Act and by Dr. Friedman, remedies to those two deficiencies would be that either monetary growth must be regulated by a Constitutional Amendment establishing either a zero (i.e., stable supply – no change) or a low fixed rate of annual growth (such as 3%) or by legislation, or, fiat money must be abolished and replaced with a commodity-based money such as gold (and/or silver or whatever a real free market develops as money).*

Unfortunately, legislation is subject to political manipulation *(such as the how CPI is currently manipulated to indicate inflation is under 2% when it is closer to 10%)* and relatively easy change, so this is not the ideal, but is of course much more easily passed. Such a Constitutional Amendment would far less subject to manipulation, as would be a commodity/gold-backed money (but even those can be manipulated in various ways) – they would be preferable to legislation. If those safeguarding elements were added, we believe this would be a huge improvement over the current system; it would in fact have the 5 advantages noted by the IMF researchers, and if bankers' back it they would be either marvelously philanthropically motivated or will have given up on their scheme's for world economic control. Neither is very likely, so *beware of any push to implement the Chicago Plan without those or similar safeguards.*

The combination of international bank control of the world economy via the BIS/IMF/World bank and State control is, as we all know, gradually heading for international totalitarianism. Any increase in power to either element is fraught with danger and must be very carefully examined (IMF paper).[24]

The Money Masters explains the history behind the current world depression and the bankers' goal of world economic control by a very small coterie of private bankers, above all governments. The Central bankers' Bank for International Settlements (BIS) in 1988 in the "Basel I" regulations imposed an 8% capital reserve standard on member central banks. This almost immediately threw Japan into a 15 year economic depression. In 2004 Basel II imposed "mark to the market" capital valuation standards that required international banks to revalue their reserves according to changing market valuations (such as falling home or stock prices). The US implemented those standards in November, 2007. In December 2007 the US stock market collapsed and

24 http://www.imf.org/external/pubs/ft/wp/2012/wp12202.pdf

credit began drying up as banks withheld loans to comply with the 8% capital requirement as collateral valuations began to drop. The snowball effect of tightening credit, which reduces economic activity and values further, which resulted in further tightening of credit, etc., has produced a worldwide depression which is worsening.

Those capital standards have not been relaxed despite the crushing effects on the world economy[25] the credit contraction it requires has caused. Why? Because: "The purpose of this financial crisis is to take down the U.S. dollar as the stable datum of planetary

---

25 The U.S did modify these rules somewhat a year after the devastation had taken place here, but the rules are still fully in place in the rest of the world and the results are appalling. "The powers of financial capitalism had a far-reaching plan, nothing less than to create a world system of financial control in private hands able to dominate the political system of each country and the economy of the world as a whole... Their secret is that they have annexed from governments, monarchies, and republics the power to create the world's money..." .- Prof. Carroll Quigley renowned, late Georgetown macro-historian (mentioned by former President Clinton in his first nomination acceptance speech), author of Tragedy and Hope. "He [Carroll Quigley] was one of the last great macro-historians who traced the development of civilization...with an awesome capability." – Dr. Peter F. Krogh, Dean of the School of Foreign Service (Georgetown).

finance and, in the midst of the resulting confusion, put in its place a Global Monetary Authority [GMA - run directly by international bankers freed of any government control] -a planetary financial control organization"- Bruce Wiseman

The Two Step Plan to National Economic Reform and Recovery

1. Direct the Treasury Department to issue U.S. Notes (like Lincoln's Greenbacks; can also be in electronic deposit format) to pay off the National debt.

2. Increase the reserve ratio private banks are required to maintain from 10% to 100%, thereby terminating their ability to create money, while simultaneously absorbing the funds created to retire the national debt.

These two relatively simple steps, which Congress has the power to enact, would extinguish the national debt, without inflation or deflation, and *end the unjust practice of private banks creating money as loans (i.e., fractional reserve banking)*. Paying off the national debt would wipe out the $400+ billion annual interest payments and thereby balance the budget. This Act would stabilize the economy and end the boom-bust economic cycles caused by fractional reserve banking. *The monetarist school, of which Dr. Milton Friedman was the acknowledged head, has been rightly criticized by the Austrian school of economics for failing to recognize and deal with the fact that no fiat money system has ever lasted long before the government instituting it succumbed to the temptation to inflate the money supply as an indirect tax on the people, proportionately decreasing the value of their savings and wages, and transferring their wealth into the hands of the government.* This is certainly a valid critique. The so-called "Great Recession" beginning in 2007, TARP, QE1, QE2 etc. and the staggering increase in the national debt has proven the validity of that critique – the Austrian school was right.

To be fair to Dr. Friedman, he did write that "we do need a commitment to sound money. The best arrangement currently would be to require the monetary authorities to keep the percentage rate of growth of the monetary base within a fixed range. This is a particularly difficult amendment to draft because it is so closely linked to the particular institutional structure. One version would be: Congress shall have the power to authorize non-interest-bearing obligations of the government in the form of currency or book entries, provided that the total dollar amount outstanding increases by no more than 5 percent per year and no less than 3 percent."

However, given the near-impossibility of passing such a Constitutional Amendment, it can fairly be argued that Dr. Friedman really had no practical means (only the theoretical one, above) to offer to restraint the government from debasing the currency and inflating away the wealth of the people. *That being so, we part company with Dr. Friedman's conclusion that "It is neither feasible nor desirable to restore a gold-or-silver coin standard."* Again, to be fair to him, Dr. Friedman later softened his stance against gold and stated that it would be preferable to what we have, a fractional reserve banking system. To that shift in thought, we say, Amen. The Money Masters website will be updating information and the Monetary Reform Act to explain the Austrian school's solution to the current economic crisis in the light of events the last 5 years. One thing both schools of economic thought agree upon, as does Dr. Ron Paul: End the Fed!

"Banking was conceived in iniquity and was born in sin. The bankers own the earth. Take it away from them, but leave them the power to create money, and with the flick of the pen they will create enough deposits to buy it back again. However, take it away from them, and all the great fortunes like mine will disappear and they ought to disappear, for this would be a happier and better world to live in. But, if you wish to remain the slaves of bankers and pay the cost of your own slavery, let them continue to create money."

"But if you want to continue to be slaves of the banks and pay the cost of your own slavery, then let bankers continue to create money and control credit."

Josiah Stamp

Reviews of the *Money Masters* Documentary

Mr. Carmack, What you have shown in the scenario is what we are constantly doing at the personal level as well as the public level. It is the policy of exploitation that the rich employ against the poor. This is why grandfather [Mahatma Gandhi] said 'Materialism and morality have an inverse relationship – when one increases the other decreases.' If I may, I would like to keep the videos as resource material to teach students about economic violence in the world. With good wishes. Yours sincerely, Arun Gandhi, M.K. Gandhi Institute for Nonviolence"

"Mr. Carmack, As you know, I am entirely sympathetic with the objectives of your Monetary Reform Act...You deserve a great deal of credit for carrying through so thoroughly on your own conception...I am impressed by your persistence and attention to detail in your successive revisions... Best wishes. Milton Friedman," Nobel Laureate in Economics; Senior Fellow, Hoover Institution on War, Revolution and Peace

"Compelling! Excellently produced and impressively documented. If you want to learn what our Founding Fathers and Presidents have to say about money and its control, you will want to see [The Money Masters]..."- Dr. D. James Kennedy, Coral Ridge.

"I endorse the video because people should know what is happening." – Malachi Martin, late Professor at the Pontifical Biblical Institute and a close associate of Pope John XXIII; author of: The Windswept House; Vatican; The Keys of the Blood.

G. Edward Griffin, author of The Creature From Jekyll Island; A Second Look at the Federal Reserve. "I appreciate and applaud your efforts to accomplish something specific in the area of monetary reform. . . I do not hesitate to recommend that people view The Money Masters for the excellent overview of fraudulent banking which it presents. . . "

"This is undoubtedly the most comprehensive presentation of the history of our money system and who is responsible for the disastrous consequences that has left us with an unconstitutional money system and multi-trillion dollar debt." - Dr. W. Cleon Skousen, author of The Naked Capitalist and The Naked Communist

APPENDIX 2

The FED: Lies, Thievery, and Deceit,
by Dr. Ken Matto[26]

The Federal Reserve System became the central bank of the United States through deceit in 1913. The idea came about on a meeting in Jekyll Island off the coast of Georgia in 1910. The bankers in this country, especially J.P. Morgan, created a currency panic in 1907 in order to get the American people to accept the idea of a central bank.

A central bank already existed in England from as far back as 1694. The Rothschilds completely dominate

---

26 https://www.scionofzion.com/federalreserve.htm;
    https://forum.woodenboat.com The Bilge;
    https://www.onepoliticalplaza.com/t-13319-1.html;
    https://hotcopper.com.au/threads/the-federal-reserve-history-
    of-lies-thievery.1663181/, to name but a few sites

the banking system. It is estimated their wealth goes into the trillions.

Baron Nathan Mayer Rothschild boasted: "I care not what puppet is placed upon the throne of England to rule the Empire on which the sun never sets. The man that controls Britain's money supply controls the British Empire, and I control the British money supply."

The idea of a central bank is to so enslave the people of the country to a debt money system that you continue to collect taxes continuously which just covers the interest. *The duped people of the United States are paying about $400 billion dollars per year to the IRS which is the collection agency for the Federal Reserve.*

Total FED controlled amount per year = debt + military = 229+598=$827 billion/year=1.26% FED assets on paper. This implies the FED had a total GP-on-paper (consolidated assets) of $66 trillion in 2015. Borrowing=$583 billion/year. Hence: without FED, US would have a surplus of $244 billion per year.

Lie: the current federal funds rate rose to **2.5 percent** when the Federal Open Market Committee met on December 19, 2018. This benchmark rate is an indicator of the economy's health.

During the time of the Babylonian captivity of Judah, a man named Jacob Egibi became the founding father of modern banking. While Judah was in captivity, Jacob began a business of loaning out money for a rate of interest. During the Reign of King Kandalanu of Babylon (circa 648-625 B.C.) a new phenomenon appeared on the scene which Jacob Egibi played a major part, and that was the invention of private banking. There were 2 prominent families at this time, they were the Egibi family and the Iranu families. These 2 families are not a figment of imagination as their names have appeared in many cuneiform tablets discovered by Archaeologists. It is believed that the Egibi family was taken with the first captivity into Assyria and then later migrated to Babylon. At the time of the 70 year captivity, Jacob Egibi already had an ongoing private banking business in which he collected large sums of interest. *Now we have secular insight as to why many of the Jews did not want to return with Nehemiah to rebuild the temple at Jerusalem.*

During the time of the Persian period, loan sharking became a business where interest rates of anywhere from 30-50% were charged. As time went on, the writings of the Roman historian Tacitus, tells us that during the reigns of Caesar Augustus (27 BC - 14 AD) and Tiberius (14-32 AD) records of the Roman empire reveal deposits, withdrawals, brokers fees and loans. When the western Roman Empire fell, banking continued to thrive in Egypt, Byzantium, and the Arab nations of the Red Sea.

When the Christian era began to take hold and the church became a powerful entity, she returned to the Old Testament Edict of not charging usury and this idea continued up until the time of the Renaissance when banks began appearing across Europe. To show you how some kings despised usury, I offer 2 quotations:

Alfred the Great, King of England; 849-901: "...if any man is found taking usury, his lands will be confiscated, and he will be banished from England..."

James 1, King of England; 1566-1625: "...If a man is found taking usury, his lands will be confiscated. It is like taking a man's life, and it must not be tolerated..."

With the rise of international trade which commenced at the end of the medieval period, many of the banks were allowed to coin money for their transactions. At that time, there was no such thing as national money and when the banks minted coins, they were all of different value which created a dilemma for international trade. The first "Christian" gold coins were struck by Emperor Frederick II in 1225 A.D. Then came the "ducats'' of Portugal, the "florins" of Florence, the "agnels" of France, and the "sequins" which became the official coins of Genoa and Venice. Europe then progressed from the Feudal system and with this came trade between different nations which resulted in foreign moneys accumulating in the various cities in Europe.

1694: The Year which Doomed the World's Economies

The government of King William III was in desperate need of money. When learning of this situation, a man named William Patterson put together a cartel of wealthy men, of which he was the leader. Patterson and cronies agreed to loan the King 1,200,000 pound sterling which would have been approximately 6 million dollars at 8% interest per annum on the condition that the king would grant 2 things:

1) He would grant Patterson and his associates a charter which would name them "The Bank of England," and

2) This bank shall have the "sole and exclusive right" to issue notes to the fullest extent of its capital.

The people were having a problem with their gold and silver coins of which the bankers quickly came to the rescue. The solution is aptly described by Professor Carroll Quigley in his book, *Tragedy and Hope:*

...for generations men had sought to avoid the one drawback of gold, its heaviness, by using pieces of paper to represent specific pieces of gold. Today we call such pieces of paper "gold certificates." Such a certificate entitled its bearer to exchange it for pieces of gold on demand, but in view of convenience of paper, only a small fraction of certificate holders ever did make such demands. It early became clear that gold need be held on hand only to the amount needed to cover the fraction of certificates likely to be presented for payment; accordingly the rest of the gold could be used for business purposes, or, what amounts to the same thing. *A volume of certificates could be issued greater than the volume of gold reserved for payment....Such an excess volume of paper claims against reserves we now call bank notes.*

In effect, this creation of paper claims greater than the reserves available means that bankers were creating money out of nothing...

The King literally granted the Bank of England the legal right to print all the money that would be used in commerce by the people and the government. In other words the Bank of England became the sole money source of any currency that was used in English commerce by either the people or the government. If they needed more money, they simply printed it. It is said that by 1698 British government owed 16 million pounds sterling to the Bank of England. Keep in mind this was only 4 years.

1773: The Second Date of Infamy

In 1773, a wealthy goldsmith and coin dealer named Mayer Amschel Bauer (1743-1812) summoned 12 wealthy and influential men to his place of business in Frankfurt, Germany. His purpose for the meeting was to impress upon these men that if they pooled their resources, it was possible to gain control of the wealth, natural resources, and manpower of the entire world.

He then outlined a 25 point plan on how to accomplish
it.

Those 25 points are:

1. Use violence and terrorism rather than academic
discussions.

2. Preach Liberalism to usurp political power.

3. Initiate class warfare.

4. Politicians must be cunning and deceptive â€" any
moral code leaves a politician vulnerable.

5. Dismantle existing forces of order and regulation.
Reconstruct all existing institutions.

6. Remain invisible until the very moment when it has
gained such strength that no cunning or force can
undermine it.

7. Use Mob Psychology to control the masses. Without
absolute despotism one cannot rule efficiently.

8. Advocate the use of alcoholic liquors, drugs, moral
corruption and all forms of vice, used systematically
by agenteurs to corrupt the youth.

9. Seize properties by any means to secure submission
and sovereignty.

10. Foment wars and control the peace conferences so
that neither of the combatants gains territory placing
them further in debt and therefore into our power.

11. Choose candidates for public office who will be servile and obedient to our commands, so they may be readily used as pawns in our game.

12. Use the Press for propaganda to control all outlets of public information, while remaining in the shadows, clear of blame.

13. Make the masses believe they had been the prey of criminals. Then restore order to appear as the saviors.

14. Create financial panics. Use hunger to control to subjugate the masses.

15. Infiltrate Freemasonry to take advantage of the Grand Orient Lodges to cloak the true nature of their work in philanthropy. Spread their atheistic-materialistic ideology amongst the Goyim (gentiles).

16. When the hour strikes for our sovereign lord of the entire World to be crowned, their influence will banish everything that might stand in his way.

17. Use systematic deception, high-sounding phrases and popular slogans. The opposite of what has been promised can always be done afterwards... That is of no consequence.

18. A Reign of Terror is the most economical way to bring about speedy subjection.

19. Masquerade as political, financial and economic advisers to carry out our mandates with Diplomacy and without fear of exposing the secret power behind national and international affairs.

20. Ultimate world government is the goal. It will be necessary to establish huge monopolies, so even the largest fortunes of the Goyim will depend on us to such an extent that they will go to the bottom together with the credit of their governments on the day after the great political smash.

21. Use economic warfare. Rob the "Goyim" of their landed properties and industries with a combination of high taxes and unfair competition.

22. Make the Goyim destroy each other so there will only be the proletariat left in the world, with a few millionaires devoted to our cause, and sufficient police and soldiers to protect our interest.

23. Call it The New Order. Appoint a Dictator.

24. Fool, bemuse and corrupt the younger members of society by teaching them theories and principles we know to be false.

25 Twist national and international laws into a contradiction which first masks the law and

afterwards hides it altogether. Substitute arbitration for law.

The plan was put into operation and evidentiary information exists that Bauer aligned himself with Adam Weishaupt who was the founder of the Illuminati whose aim was and still is world domination. Bauer later changed his name to Rothschild which means "red shield." He took it from the red sign which hung outside his place of business. The eagle was clutching 5 golden arrows in its claws. It was supposed to symbolize his five sons. Presently the red shield represents the official coat of arms of the city of Frankfurt, Germany.

Later on each of the five sons were dispatched to a major city in Europe to establish a branch of the Rothschild banking firm.

Son #1 - Amschel - Remained in Frankfurt and propelled Germany to financial success under Bismarck.

Son #2 - Salomon - Went to Vienna, Austria. he became a leader in the Austria-Hungary Empire.

Son #3 - Nathan Mayer - Went to England where he took control of the Bank of England.

Son #4 - Carl - Went to Naples where he became the most powerful man in Italy through his banking skills.

Son #5 - James Jacob - Went to Paris where he established the central bank. He was credited with dominating the financial destiny of the nation of France.

By 1850, the House of Rothschild represented more wealth than all the families of Europe. Shortly after he formed the Bank of England, William Patterson lost control of it to Nathan Rothschild and here is how he did it:

• *Nathan Rothschild was an observer on the day the Duke of Wellington defeated Napoleon at Waterloo. He knew that with this information he could make a fortune. He later paid a sailor a big fee to take him across the English Channel in bad weather. The news of Napoleon's defeat would take a while to hit England. When Nathan arrived in London, he began selling securities and bonds in a panic. The other investors were deceived into believing that Napoleon won the war and was eyeing England so they began to sell their securities too. What they were unaware of is that Rothschild's agents were buying all the securities that were being sold in panic. In one day, the Rothschild* fortune grew by one million pounds. They literally bought control of England for a few cents on the dollar. The same way the Rockefeller's went into Japan after World War 2 and bought everything 10 cents on the dollar.

e.g. SONY=Standard Oil New York, a Rockefeller Company.

Frederick Morton wrote in his book, "The Rothschilds":

"...the wealth of the Rothschilds consists of the bankruptcy of nations."

There were other wealthy families in Europe and America which were allowed to join "the international banking club" such as John D. Rockefeller and John Pierpont Morgan.

Early American Wisdom

The Americans had won their political independence but their financial independence was in jeopardy. The international bankers had an agent in place and his name was Alexander Hamilton who wanted a central bank. Thomas Jefferson lobbied vehemently against the central bank stating it was contrary to the Constitution. However, a central bank was formed in 1781 known as the Bank of North America which was patterned after the Bank of England. The colonists wanted nothing to do with it so it folded in 1790. The international bankers countered the closing of the Bank of North America by gaining a charter for the Bank of the United States which was chartered on February 25, 1791. The Bank of France desired the formation of the US Bank also and it was chartered for 20 years.

In 1826, the second bank's charter was soon to expire and presidential candidate Andrew Jackson campaigned strongly against a central bank which was owned and operated by the international banking element. Here is Jackson's opinion of those bankers:

"You are a den of vipers. I intend to wipe you out, and by the Eternal God I will rout you out...If people only understood the rank injustice of the money and banking system, there would be a revolution by morning."

In 1836, the charter did expire but that was not the end of the international banking influence in this country. *The Civil War was planned in England as far back as 1809. Slavery was not the real cause of the Civil War. The Rothschilds (who were heavy into the slave trade) used the slavery issue as "a divide and conquer strategy" which almost split the United States in two. The Bank of England financed the North while the Paris branch of the Rothschild bank funded the South. In 1863, the National Banking Act was passed despite protest by President Lincoln.* This act allowed a private corporation the authority to issue our money.

Enter 1913

In November of 1910, some of these vultures came together at the Jekyl Island Hunt Club on Jekyl Island, Georgia. What were they hunting? The biggest prize of all, the absolute and complete control of all the money in America which means control of all America and with it the power to make slaves of all the people.

Those who attended were: Senator Nelson Aldrich (Nelson Rockefeller's maternal grandfather); A. Piatt Andrew, Economist and Assistant Secretary of the Treasury; Frank Vanderlip, President of the National City Bank of New York; Henry P. Norton, President of Morgan's First National Bank of New York; Paul Moritz Warburg, a German who was partner in the New York banking house of Kuhn, Loeb Co.; Benjamin Strong, an aid to J. P. Morgan.

Paul Warburg was credited as the architect of the bill which was passed by Congress and signed by traitorous Woodrow Wilson. It was entitled the Federal Reserve Act of 1913. America once again had a central bank but this time they had placed America under an absolute dictatorship. *President James Garfield had insight into this situation:* "It must be realized that whoever controls the volume of money in any country is absolutely master of all industry commerce."

The Federal Reserve was incorporated in 1914 and has been creating a completely unnecessary national debt ever since. In simple terms, the Fed creates money as debt. They create money out of thin air by nothing more than a book entry. Whenever the members of the Fed make any loans, that debt money is our money supply.

The United States went bankrupt in 1938 because of this system. It took the Fed only 25 years to bankrupt the USA. Can you imagine how little time it would take these vultures to bankrupt a developing nation? The American people are paying about $300 billion dollars a year in interest to this phony organization. *When you look in the Washington, D.C. phone book, you will not find the Federal Reserve in the Government section as they are a private concern.*

The national debt is increased about $1.71 billion dollars every day (as of October 12, 2004) . Have you taken a look at your money? It says "Federal Reserve Note" which means it is an instrument of debt. There is no real money in circulation.

The Assassination of President Kennedy

One of the greatest cover-ups in history was the Killing of the President. If you believe the Mafia did it, then I have ocean front land in Kansas for you to buy. President Kennedy was murdered over money, worth $4 billion. You see, he had printed $4 billion worth of non-interest bearing money which meant he began to chop at the profits of the vultures. *Interest-free money means the national debt is eliminated and the power of the international banking element is broken.* So to prevent Kennedy from abolishing the illegal Fed, he was assassinated. Coincidence? As soon as the *traitor Johnson* was in office, he recalled all the debt free notes and continued our country in the same path of ruin. There, the mystery of the killing is over. Just follow the trail of the money.

War

Now that the Federal Reserve was firmly in place, schemes had to be constructed to get the government to borrow so a continuously growing national debt would happen. So here are some coincidences: The Federal Reserve is created in 1913, then in 1914 we have World War 1. *Right at the end of World War 1, we have a depressed economy especially in the Weimar Republic where 2 billion marks could buy a loaf of bread.* In 1917, we had the Bolshevik revolution in Russia. A man named Lord Alfred Milner was a front man and paymaster for the Rothschilds in Petrograd during the revolution. He later headed a secret organization called The Round Table which was dedicated to a one world government run by wealthy financiers under socialism.

Then, lo and behold, in the 1920's we see a little known corporal with 12 men meeting in a beer hall in Munich while in America the Roaring 20's were in progress until *October, 1929. Then the Federal Reserve withheld money from circulation so bills could not be* paid, *while simultaneously they were calling in all their loans which caused the stock market to crash.* By 1932 the price of stocks had plummeted 80%. When the bankers plunged this nation into a depression on that fateful day in October, at the New York Stock Exchange was a visitor, his name was Winston Churchill who stated after the crash of '29, "Now I know who wields the real power." The key to understanding the Great Depression is to realize that when the Federal Reserve had contracted the money supply, there was not enough money in circulation to pay bills, to hire people, to pay back loans, etc. The crash of the stock market was the symptom but the cause was the Fed restricting the money supply. This is their weapon which is used today. When they flood the country with money, this causes inflation.

Then we come into the 1930's and the rise of Hitler. Hitler was also funded by Wall Street through the Industrialist I.G. Farben. Let's test the theory of *follow the money.* Here is a little known corporal with no money meeting in a beer hall in Munich with only about 12 men. In a seriously depressed and defeated country, there begins to rise another military dictatorship. By 1934 the Nuremberg Rallies were in

place and Germany was rebuilt. In that countries'
economy who had that much money to rebuild Germany
into a powerful country which marched across Europe
and almost defeated Russia in the first 24 hours of
Case White (The invasion of Russia)? The answer is the
bankers of the USA and England. *In fact, a banker
named Bernard Baruch was President Roosevelt's
personal advisor during World War 2. Baruch made
$200 million dollars as a result of World War 2. During
WW2 the Rockefellers were selling oil to the Germans
from their Standard Oil concern in Argentina.*

*The Council on Foreign Relations (CFR) was formed in
1919 in Paris, France by Colonel Edward Mandell House
who was known as Woodrow Wilson's alter ego. The
CFR was and still is dedicated to the one world rule
under a new world order. In fact, every war has been
planned by the CFR. Every American President since
1919 has had their cabinet filled with CFR members.
Also our traitorous Presidents fill their cabinets with
not only CFR members but those of the Trilateral
Commission, the Bilderbergers, the Yale Fraternity of
the Skull and Bones (George Bush was a member of
this).*

These members insure that the will of the bankers is done, even if the President is not a member of any group. *After WW2, was fought another war was created known as the Korean War (which was started by a phone call from John Foster Dulles), then the Vietnam War. During the Vietnamese War, the Rockefellers had a metals processing plant going full blast in North Vietnam. The Rockefellers have the blood of thousands of Americans on their hands because of their supplying the Russians with weapons and metals. The North Vietnamese received their weapons from Russia. The only reason these rats are never indicted for treason, is because since WW2 there has never been a declared war which means if we have no official enemy, there can be no aiding the enemy AKA treason.*

Presently we have skirmishes such as the Gulf War of 1990 which was an experiment by the New World Order crowd to see how fast they can assemble an army in case a country does not choose to obey the dictates of the banker bosses. Of course funding for the gulf war came from borrowing money from the Fed. Wherever you hear of a limited war, or some type of political destabilization, think of the money trail. Wars are started in foreign countries, then our President goes there and gives millions of dollars of borrowed money which normally goes into the pockets of the dictators. Nowhere in our Constitution is it written that our government is to borrow money and give it away.

Final Thoughts

The American economy has been sucked dry by the Federal Reserve System. Americans think they own property but the truth is the entire United States has been mortgaged to the bankers. The Rothschilds and Rockefellers become richer while the peoples of the world become poorer. The International Monetary Fund and the World Bank are also designed to loan money to developing nations with the understanding that they will never be able to repay so with every loan made to a country, it becomes their death knell. *The entire world has been plunged into a debt economy which means 6 billion people are in debt to about 250 men. But keep in mind that all their wealth is phony because it is created money without any gold backing.*
I really laugh when Wall Street bows down to Ben Bernanke who is nothing more than a boot licker of the

International Banking element who takes his orders by phone too. So many people rejoice when the Federal Reserve has a policy meeting and no interest rate increase happens. The truth is that we should never have a Federal Reserve to begin with. They print money, loan it into circulation, and the American people are strapped with more debt.

I remember leaving materials on the Federal Reserve at a meeting of Concerned Women for America. The next day I went back and not one copy was taken. The reason given me was because it was not approved material. *Groups like Concerned Women for America and the Christian Coalition and Rush Limbaugh are something known as controlled opposition.* They are allowed to exist as long as they do not bring up the real issues. If they stick to the created liberal Democrat Vs. conservative Republican agenda, they can exist and the bankers will even make them famous. But you will never hear a Beverly LaHaye, Tim LaHaye, Jim Dobson, Billy Graham, Gary Bauer, or any other famous Christians ever tackle the real issues like the illegal Fed which causes all the poverty in every country. If these people would think for a minute that if $350 billion dollars a year was not being sucked out of the economy and was used for the people in this country, we would surely have enough to help other nations and our own problems. *Crime would almost be non-existent with a monetized money system.* The Great Commission would also be funded without worrying if there will be enough left over to feed the children.

The Federal Reserve is an independent entity established by the Federal Reserve Act of 1913. At that time, President Wilson wanted a government-appointed central board. But Congress wanted the Fed to have 12 regional banks to represent America's diverse regions. The compromise meant the Fed has both.

Below one finds a list of the principal nine member banks of the FRS, who control all the others. In spite of the diversity of names, they are all owned by the Rothschilds.

THE NINE MEMBER BANKS OF THE FEDERAL
RESERVE

Rothschild Bank of London
Warburg Bank of Hamburg
Rothschild Bank of Berlin
Kuhn Loeb & Lehman Brothers of New York
Lazard Brothers of Paris
Israel Moses Seif Banks of Italy
Goldman Sachs Bank of New York
Warburg Bank of Amsterdam
Chase Manhattan Bank of New York

APPENDIX 3

Eight Mafia Families
by Dean Henderson,[27] June 2018

Abstract: Companies under Rockefeller control include Exxon Mobil, Chevron Texaco, BP Amoco, Marathon Oil, Freeport McMoran, Quaker Oats, ASARCO, United, Delta, Northwest, ITT, International Harvester, Xerox, Boeing, Westinghouse, Hewlett-Packard, Honeywell, International Paper, Pfizer, Motorola, Monsanto, Union Carbide and General Foods. Bretton Woods was a boon to the Eight Families. The IMF and World Bank were central to this "new world order".

---

27 http://www.hannenabintuherland.com/europe/the-federal-reserve-cartel-the-eight-families-who-own-the-usa-the-rise-of-bis-imf-world-bank-dean-henderson-on-free21-org/

The Four Horsemen of Banking (Bank of America, JP Morgan Chase, Citigroup and Wells Fargo) own the Four Horsemen of Oil (Exxon Mobil, Royal Dutch/Shell, BP and Chevron Texaco); in tandem with Deutsche Bank, BNP, Barclays and other European old money behemoths. Their monopoly over the global economy does not end at the edge of the oil patch. According to company 10K filings to the SEC, the Four Horsemen of Banking are among the top ten stock holders of virtually every Fortune 500 corporation. (Photo: Now News)

So who then are the stockholders in these money center banks? This information is guarded much more closely. My queries to bank regulatory agencies regarding stock ownership in the top 25 US bank holding companies were given Freedom of Information Act status, before being denied on "national security" grounds.

This is rather ironic, since many of the bank's stockholders reside in Europe. One important repository for the wealth of the global oligarchy that owns these bank holding companies is US Trust Corporation – founded in 1853 and now owned by Bank of America. A recent US Trust Corporate Director and Honorary Trustee was Walter Rothschild.

DAVID ROCKEFELLER

Some even believe we are part of a secret cabal working against the best interests of the United States, characterizing my family and me as 'internationalists' and of conspiring with others around the world to build a more integrated global political and economic structure — one world, if you will.

If that's the charge, I stand guilty, and I am proud of it.

- David Rockefeller

Other directors included Daniel Davison of JP Morgan Chase, Richard Tucker of Exxon Mobil, Daniel Roberts of Citigroup and Marshall Schwartz of Morgan Stanley. J. W. McCallister, an oil industry insider with House of Saud connections, wrote in The Grim Reaper that information he acquired from Saudi bankers cited 80% ownership of the New York Federal Reserve Bank- by far the most powerful Fed branch- by just eight families, four of which reside in the US.

They are the Goldman Sachs, Rockefellers, Lehmans and Kuhn Loebs of New York; the Rothschilds of Paris and London; the Warburgs of Hamburg; the Lazards of Paris; and the Israel Moses Seifs of Rome.

CPA Thomas D. Schauf corroborates McCallister's claims, adding that ten banks control all twelve Federal Reserve Bank branches. He names N.M. Rothschild of London, Rothschild Bank of Berlin, Warburg Bank of Hamburg, Warburg Bank of Amsterdam, Lehman Brothers of New York, Lazard Brothers of Paris, Kuhn Loeb Bank of New York, Israel Moses Seif Bank of Italy, Goldman Sachs of New York and JP Morgan Chase Bank of New York.

Schauf lists William Rockefeller, Paul Warburg, Jacob Schiff and James Stillman as individuals who own large shares of the Fed. The Schiffs are insiders at Kuhn Loeb. The Stillmans are Citigroup insiders, who married into the Rockefeller clan at the turn of the century. Eustace Mullins came to the same conclusions in his book *The Secrets of the Federal Reserve*, in which he displays charts connecting the Fed and its member banks to the families of Rothschild, Warburg, Rockefeller and the others.

The control that these banking families exert over the global economy cannot be overstated and is quite intentionally shrouded in secrecy. Their corporate media arm is quick to discredit any information exposing this private central banking cartel as "conspiracy theory". Yet the facts remain.

The House of Morgan The Federal Reserve Bank was born in 1913, the same year US banking scion J. Pierpont Morgan died and the Rockefeller Foundation was formed. The House of Morgan presided over American finance from the corner of Wall Street and Broad, acting as quasi-US central bank since 1838, when George Peabody founded it in London.

Peabody was a business associate of the Rothschilds. In 1952 Fed researcher Eustace Mullins put forth the supposition that the Morgans were nothing more than

Rothschild agents. Mullins wrote that the Rothschilds, "...preferred to operate anonymously in the US behind the facade of J.P. Morgan & Company". Author Gabriel Kolko stated, "Morgan's activities in 1895-1896 in selling US gold bonds in Europe were based on an alliance with the House of Rothschild." The Morgan financial octopus wrapped its tentacles quickly around the globe. Morgan Grenfell operated in London. Morgan et Ce ruled Paris. The Rothschild's Lambert cousins set up Drexel & Company in Philadelphia.

The House of Morgan catered to the Astors, DuPonts, Guggenheims, Vanderbilts and Rockefellers. It financed the launch of AT&T, General Motors, General Electric and DuPont. Like the London-based Rothschild and Barings banks, Morgan became part of the power structure in many countries.

By 1890 the House of Morgan was lending to Egypt's central bank, financing Russian railroads, floating Brazilian provincial government bonds and funding Argentine public works projects. A recession in 1893 enhanced Morgan's power. That year Morgan saved the US government from a bank panic, forming a syndicate to prop up government reserves with a shipment of $62 million worth of Rothschild gold. Morgan was the driving force behind Western expansion in the US, financing and controlling West-bound railroads through voting trusts.

In 1879 Cornelius Vanderbilt's Morgan-financed New York Central Railroad gave preferential shipping rates to John D. Rockefeller's budding Standard Oil monopoly, cementing the Rockefeller/Morgan relationship. The House of Morgan now fell under Rothschild and Rockefeller family control.

A New York Herald headline read, "Railroad Kings Form Gigantic Trust". *J. Pierpont Morgan, who once stated, "Competition is a sin", now opined gleefully, "Think of it. All competing railroad traffic west of St. Louis placed in the control of about thirty men."* Morgan and Edward Harriman's banker Kuhn Loeb held a monopoly over the railroads, while banking dynasties Lehman, Goldman Sachs and Lazard joined the Rockefellers in controlling the US industrial base.

In 1903 Banker's Trust was set up by the Eight Families. Benjamin Strong of Banker's Trust was the first Governor of the New York Federal Reserve Bank. The 1913 creation of the Fed fused the power of the Eight Families to the military and diplomatic might of the US government. If their overseas loans went unpaid, the oligarchs could now deploy US Marines to collect the debts. Morgan, Chase and Citibank formed an international lending syndicate. The House of Morgan was cozy with the British House of Windsor and the Italian House of Savoy. The Kuhn Loebs, Warburgs, Lehmans, Lazards, Israel Moses Seifs and Goldman Sachs also had close ties to European royalty. By 1895 Morgan controlled the flow of gold in and out of the US. The first American wave of mergers was in its infancy and was being promoted by the bankers. In 1897 there were sixty-nine industrial mergers. By 1899 there were twelve-hundred. In 1904 John Moody –founder of Moody's Investor Services– said it was impossible to talk of Rockefeller and Morgan interests as separate.

Public distrust of the combine spread

Many considered them traitors working for European old money. Rockefeller's Standard Oil, Andrew Carnegie's US Steel and Edward Harriman's railroads were all financed by banker Jacob Schiff at Kuhn Loeb, who worked closely with the European Rothschilds. Several Western states banned the bankers. Populist preacher William Jennings Bryan was thrice the Democratic nominee for President from 1896 -1908. The central theme of his anti-imperialist campaign was that America was falling into a trap of "financial servitude to British capital". Teddy Roosevelt defeated Bryan in 1908, but was forced by this spreading populist wildfire to enact the Sherman Anti-Trust Act. He then went after the Standard Oil Trust. In 1912 the Pujo hearings were held, addressing concentration of power on Wall Street.

That same year Mrs. Edward Harriman sold her substantial shares in New York's Guaranty Trust Bank to J.P. Morgan, creating Morgan Guaranty Trust. Judge Louis Brandeis convinced President Woodrow Wilson to call for an end to interlocking board directorates. In 1914 the Clayton Anti-Trust Act was passed. Jack Morgan –J. Pierpont's son and successor- responded by calling on Morgan clients Remington and Winchester to increase arms production.

He argued that the US needed to enter WWI. Goaded by the Carnegie Foundation and other oligarchy fronts, Wilson accommodated. As Charles Tansill wrote in America Goes to War, "Even before the clash of arms, the French firm of Rothschild Freres cabled to

Morgan & Company in New York suggesting the flotation of a loan of $100 million, a substantial part of which was to be left in the US to pay for French purchases of American goods."

The House of Morgan financed half the US war effort, while receiving commissions for lining up contractors like GE, Du Pont, US Steel, Kennecott and ASARCO. All were Morgan clients. Morgan also financed the British Boer War in South Africa and the Franco-Prussian War. The 1919 Paris Peace Conference was presided over by Morgan, which led both German and Allied reconstruction efforts. In the 1930's populism resurfaced in America after Goldman Sachs, Lehman Bank and others profited from the Crash of 1929.

House Banking Committee Chairman Louis McFadden (D-NY) said of the Great Depression, "It was no accident. It was a carefully contrived occurrence... The international bankers sought to bring about a condition of despair here so they might emerge as rulers of us all". Sen. Gerald Nye (D-ND) chaired a munitions investigation in 1936. Nye concluded that the House of Morgan had plunged the US into WWI to protect loans and create a booming arms industry. Nye later produced a document titled The Next War, which cynically referred to "the old goddess of democracy trick", through which Japan could be used to lure the US into WWII.

In 1937 Interior Secretary Harold Ickes warned of the influence of "America's 60 Families". Historian Ferdinand Lundberg later penned a book of the exact same title. Supreme Court Justice William O. Douglas decried, "Morgan influence...the most pernicious one in industry and finance today." Jack Morgan responded by nudging the US towards WWII. Morgan had close relations with the Iwasaki and Dan families –Japan's two wealthiest clans– who have owned Mitsubishi and Mitsui, respectively, since the companies emerged from 17th Century shogunates.

When Japan invaded Manchuria, slaughtering Chinese peasants at Nanking, Morgan downplayed the incident. Morgan also had close relations with Italian fascist Benito Mussolini, while German Nazi Dr. Hjalmer Schacht was a Morgan Bank liaison during WWII. After the war Morgan representatives met with Schacht at the Bank of International Settlements (BIS) in Basel, Switzerland. The House of Rockefeller BIS is the most powerful bank in the world, a global central bank for the Eight Families who control the private central banks of almost all Western and developing nations.

The first President of BIS was Rockefeller banker Gates McGarrah- an official at Chase Manhattan and the Federal Reserve. McGarrah was the grandfather of former CIA director Richard Helms. The Rockefellers -like the Morgans- had close ties to London. David Icke writes in Children of the Matrix, that the Rockefellers and Morgans were just "gofers" for the European Rothschilds.

BIS is owned by the Federal Reserve, Bank of England, Bank of Italy, Bank of Canada, Swiss National Bank, Nederlandsche Bank, Bundesbank and Bank of France. Historian Carroll Quigley wrote in his epic book Tragedy and Hope that BIS was part of a plan, "to create a world system of financial control in private hands able to dominate the political system of each country and the economy of the world as a whole...to be controlled in a feudalistic fashion by the central banks of the world acting in concert by secret agreements."

The US government had a historical distrust of BIS, lobbying unsuccessfully for its demise at the 1944 post-WWII Bretton Woods Conference. Instead the

Eight Families' power was exacerbated, with the Bretton Woods creation of the IMF and the World Bank.

The US Federal Reserve only took shares in BIS in September 1994. BIS holds at least 10% of monetary reserves for at least 80 of the world's central banks, the IMF and other multilateral institutions. It serves as financial agent for international agreements, collects information on the global economy and serves as lender of last resort to prevent global financial collapse. BIS promotes an agenda of monopoly capitalist fascism. It gave a bridge loan to Hungary in the 1990's to ensure privatization of that country's economy.

It served as conduit for Eight Families funding of Adolf Hitler- led by the Warburg's J. Henry Schroeder and Mendelsohn Bank of Amsterdam. Many researchers assert that BIS is at the nadir of global drug money laundering. It is no coincidence that BIS is headquartered in Switzerland, favorite hiding place for the wealth of the global aristocracy and headquarters for the P-2 Italian Freemason's Alpina Lodge and Nazi International. Other institutions which the Eight Families control include the World Economic

Forum, the International Monetary Conference and the World Trade Organization.

Bretton Woods was a boon to the Eight Families. The IMF and World Bank were central to this "new world order". In 1944 the first World Bank bonds were floated by Morgan Stanley and First Boston. The French Lazard family became more involved in House of Morgan interests. Lazard Freres –France's biggest investment bank– is owned by the Lazard and David-Weill families: old Genoese banking scions represented by Michelle Davive.

A recent Chairman and CEO of Citigroup was Sanford Weill. In 1968 Morgan Guaranty launched Euro-Clear, a Brussels-based bank clearing system for Eurodollar securities. It was the first such automated endeavor. Some took to calling Euro-Clear "The Beast". Brussels serves as headquarters for the new European Central Bank and for NATO. In 1973 Morgan officials met secretly in Bermuda to illegally resurrect the old House of Morgan, twenty years before Glass Steagal Act was repealed. Morgan and the Rockefellers provided the financial backing for Merrill Lynch, boosting it into the Big 5 of US investment banking. Merrill is now part of Bank of America.

John D. Rockefeller used his oil wealth to acquire Equitable Trust, which had gobbled up several large banks and corporations by the 1920's. The Great Depression helped consolidate Rockefeller's power. His Chase Bank merged with Kuhn Loeb's Manhattan Bank to form Chase Manhattan, cementing a long-time family relationship. The Kuhn-Loeb's had financed – along with Rothschilds – Rockefeller's quest to become king of the oil patch. National City Bank of Cleveland provided John D. with the money needed to embark upon his monopolization of the US oil industry. The bank was identified in congressional hearings as being one of three Rothschild-owned banks in the US during the 1870's, when Rockefeller first incorporated as Standard Oil of Ohio.

One Rockefeller Standard Oil partner was Edward Harkness, whose family came to control Chemical Bank. Another was James Stillman, whose family controlled Manufacturers Hanover Trust. Both banks have merged under the JP Morgan Chase umbrella. Two of James Stillman's daughters married two of William Rockefeller's sons. The two families control a big chunk of Citigroup as well. In the insurance business, the Rockefellers control Metropolitan Life, Equitable Life,

Prudential and New York Life. Rockefeller banks control 25% of all assets of the 50 largest US commercial banks and 30% of all assets of the 50 largest insurance companies. Insurance companies- the first in the US was launched by Freemasons through their Woodman's of America- play a key role in the Bermuda drug money shuffle.

Companies under Rockefeller control include Exxon Mobil, Chevron Texaco, BP Amoco, Marathon Oil, Freeport McMoran, Quaker Oats, ASARCO, United, Delta, Northwest, ITT, International Harvester, Xerox, Boeing, Westinghouse, Hewlett-Packard, Honeywell, International Paper, Pfizer, Motorola, Monsanto, Union Carbide and General Foods. The Rockefeller Foundation has close financial ties to both Ford and Carnegie Foundations. Other family philanthropic endeavors include Rockefeller Brothers Fund, Rockefeller Institute for Medical Research, General Education Board, Rockefeller University and the University of Chicago- which churns out a steady stream of far right economists as apologists for international capital, including Milton Friedman.

The family owns 30 Rockefeller Plaza, where the national Christmas tree is lighted every year, and

Rockefeller Center. *David Rockefeller was instrumental in the construction of the World Trade Center towers.*[28] The main Rockefeller family home is a hulking complex in upstate New York known as Pocantico Hills. They also own a 32-room 5th Avenue duplex in Manhattan, a mansion in Washington, DC, Monte Sacro Ranch in Venezuela, coffee plantations in Ecuador, several farms in Brazil, an estate at Seal Harbor, Maine and resorts in the Caribbean, Hawaii and Puerto Rico.

The Dulles and Rockefeller families are cousins. *Allen Dulles created the CIA, assisted the Nazis, covered up the Kennedy hit from his Warren Commission perch and struck a deal with the Muslim Brotherhood to create mind-controlled assassins. Brother John Foster Dulles presided over the phony Goldman Sachs trusts before the 1929 stock market crash and helped his brother overthrow governments in Iran and Guatemala. Both were Skull & Bones, Council on Foreign Relations (CFR) insiders and 33rd Degree Masons.*

---

[28] As explained in more detail in my book "the Snake", in the late 1990's an Israeli delegation wanted to insure the Twin Towers against terrorist attacks.

The Rockefellers were instrumental in forming the depopulation-oriented Club of Rome at their family estate in Bellagio, Italy. Their Pocantico Hills estate gave birth to the Trilateral Commission. The family is a major funder of the eugenics movement which spawned Hitler, human cloning and the current DNA obsession in US scientific circles.

John Rockefeller Jr. headed the Population Council until his death. His namesake son is a Senator from West Virginia. Brother Winthrop Rockefeller was Lieutenant Governor of Arkansas and remains the most powerful man in that state.

In an October 1975 interview with Playboy magazine, Vice-President Nelson Rockefeller —who was also Governor of New York— articulated his family's patronizing worldview, "I am a great believer in planning- economic, social, political, military, total world planning." But of all the Rockefeller brothers, it is Trilateral Commission (TC) founder and Chase Manhattan Chairman David who has spearheaded the family's fascist agenda on a global scale. He defended the Shah of Iran, the South African apartheid regime and the Chilean Pinochet junta. He was the biggest financier of the CFR, the TC and (during the Vietnam

War) the Committee for an Effective and Durable Peace in Asia- a contract bonanza for those who made their living off the conflict.

Nixon asked him to be Secretary of Treasury, but Rockefeller declined the job, knowing his power was much greater at the helm of the Chase. Author Gary Allen writes in The Rockefeller File that in 1973, "David Rockefeller met with twenty-seven heads of state, including the rulers of Russia and Red China." Following the 1975 Nugan Hand Bank/CIA coup against Australian Prime Minister Gough Whitlam, his British Crown-appointed successor Malcolm Fraser sped to the US, where he met with President Gerald Ford after conferring with David Rockefeller.

About the author: Dean Henderson[29] is the author of *Big Oil & Their Bankers in the Persian Gulf: Four Horsemen, Eight Families & Their Global Intelligence,* of *Narcotics & Terror Network* and *The Grateful Unrich: Revolution in 50 Countries.*

---

29 http://www.deanhenderson.wordpress.com

J. W. McCallister, an oil industry insider with House of Saud connections, wrote in The Grim Reaper that information he acquired from Saudi bankers cited 80% ownership of the New York Federal Reserve Bank- by far the most powerful Fed branch- by just eight families, four of which reside in the US. They are the Goldman Sachs, Rockefellers, Lehmans and Kuhn Loebs of New York; the Rothschilds of Paris and London; the Warburgs of Hamburg; the Lazards of Paris; and the Israel Moses Seifs of Rome.

APPENDIX 4

The FED is Privately Owned
by Thomas D. Schauf[30]

The Federal Reserve Bank is a Private Company

Article 1, Section 8 of the Constitution states that Congress shall have the power to coin (create) money and regulate the value thereof. Today however, the FED, which is a privately owned company, controls and profits by printing money through the Treasury, and regulating its value. The FED began with approximately 300 people or banks that became owners (stockholders

---

[30]

https://archive.org/.../The%20Federal%20Reserve%20Is%20A%20Privately%20Owne...

www.balderexlibris.com/index.php?.../Schauf-Thomas-The-Federal-Reserve-is-Private...

https://www.hannenabintuherland.com › Featured

https://famguardian.org/.../FederalReserve/Federal_Reserve_is_PRIVATELY_OWNE...

purchasing stock at $100 per share – the stock is not
publicly traded) in the Federal Reserve Banking
System. They make up an international banking cartel
of wealth beyond comparison (Reference 1, 14). The
FED banking system collects billions of dollars
(Reference 8, 17) in interest annually and distributes
the profits to its shareholders. The Congress illegally
gave the FED the right to print money (through the
Treasury) at no interest to the FED. The FED creates
money from nothing, and loans it back to us through
banks, and charges interest on our currency. The FED
also buys Government debt with money printed on a
printing press and charges U.S. taxpayers interest.
Many Congressmen and Presidents say this is fraud
(Reference 1,2,3,5,17). Who actually owns the Federal
Reserve Central Banks? The ownership of the 12
Central banks, a very well-kept secret, has been
revealed: Rothschild Bank of London Warburg Bank of
Hamburg Rothschild Bank of Berlin Lehman Brothers
of New York Lazard Brothers of Paris Kuhn Loeb Bank
of New York Israel Moses Seif Banks of Italy
Goldman, Sachs of New York Warburg Bank of
Amsterdam Chase Manhattan Bank of New York
(Reference 14, P. 13, Reference 12, P. 152) These

bankers are connected to London Banking Houses which ultimately control the FED. When England lost the Revolutionary War with America (our forefathers were fighting their own government), they planned to control us by controlling our banking system, the printing of our money, and our debt (Reference 4, 22). The individuals listed below owned banks which in turn owned shares in the FED. The banks listed below have significant control over the New York FED District, which controls the other 11 FED Districts. These banks also are partly foreign owned and control the New York FED District Bank. (Reference 22) First National Bank of New York James Stillman National City Bank, New York Mary W. Harnman National Bank of Commerce, New York A.D. Juilliard Hanover National Bank, New York Jacob Schiff Chase National Bank, New York Thomas F. Ryan Paul Warburg William Rockefeller Levi P. Morton M.T. Pyne George F. Baker Percy Pyne Mrs. G.F. St. George J.W. Sterling Katherine St. George H.P. Davidson J.P. Morgan (Equitable Life/Mutual Life) Edith Brevour T. Baker (Reference 4 for above, Reference 22 has details, P. 92, 93, 96, 179)

How did it happen?

After previous attempts to push the Federal Reserve
Act through Congress, a group of bankers funded and
staffed Woodrow Wilson's campaign for President. He
had committed to sign this act. In 1913, a Senator,
Nelson   Aldrich,   maternal   grandfather   to   the
Rockefellers, pushed the Federal Reserve Act through
Congress   just   before   Christmas   when   much   of
Congress was on vacation (Reference 3, 4, 5). When
elected,   Wilson   passed   the   FED.   Later,   Wilson
remorsefully replied (referring to the FED), "I have
unwittingly ruined my country" (Reference 17, P. 31).
Now   the   banks   financially   back   sympathetic
candidates. Not surprisingly, most of these candidates
are elected (Reference 1, P. 208-210, Reference 12, P.
235,   Reference   14,   P.   36).   The   bankers   employ
members of the Congress on weekends (nickname T&T
club -out Thursday...-in Tuesday) with lucrative
salaries (Reference 1, P. 209). Additionally, the FED
started buying up the media in the 1930's and now
owns or significantly influences most of it Reference
3, 10, 11, P. 145). Presidents Lincoln, Jackson, and
Kennedy tried to stop this family of bankers by
printing U.S. dollars without charging the taxpayers

interest (Reference 4). Today, if the government runs a deficit, the FED prints dollars through the U.S. Treasury, buys the debt, and the dollars are circulated into the economy. In 1992, taxpayers paid the FED banking system $286 billion in interest on debt the FED purchased by printing money virtually cost free (Reference 12, P. 265). Forty percent of our personal federal income taxes goes to pay this interest. The FED's books are not open to the public. Congress has yet to audit it. Congressman Wright Patman was Chairman of the House of Representatives Committee on Banking and Currency for 40 years. For 20 of those years, he introduced legislation to repeal the Federal Reserve Banking Act of 1913. Congressman Henry Gonzales, Chairman of a banking committee, introduces legislation to repeal the Federal Reserve Banking Act of 1913 nearly every year. It's always defeated, the media remains silent, and the public never learns the truth. The same bankers who own the FED control the media and give huge political contributions to sympathetic members of Congress (Reference 12, P. 155-163, Reference 22, P. 158, 159, 166). *The fed fears the population will become aware of this fraud and demand change.* We, the People, are at fault for being passive and allowing this to continue. Rep. Louis T. McFadden (R. Pa.) rose from office boy to become cashier and then President of the First National Bank in Canton Ohio. For 12 years he served as Chairman of the Committee on Banking and Currency, making him one of the foremost financial authorities in America. He fought continuously for fiscal integrity and a return to constitutional government (Reference 1). The following are portions of Rep. McFadden's speech, quoted from the Congressional Record, pages 12595-12603:

"the federal reserve board, a government board, has cheated the governmentof the united states and the people of the united states out of enough money to pay the national debt. The depredations and the iniquities of the Federal Reserve Board and the Federal Reserve banks acting together have cost this country enough money to pay the national debt several times over."

About the Federal Reserve banks, Rep. McFadden said, "They are private credit monopolies which prey upon the people of the United States for the benefit of themselves and their foreign customers; foreign and domestic speculators and swindlers; the rich and predatory money lenders. This is an era of economic misery and for the reasons that caused that misery, the Federal Reserve Board and the Federal Reserve banks are fully liable." On the subject of media control he state, "Half a million dollars was spent on one part of the propaganda organized by those same European bankers for the purpose of misleading public opinion in regard to it." Rep. McFadden continued, "Every effort has been made by the Federal Reserve Board to conceal its power but the truth is the Federal Reserve Board has usurped the government of the united states. It controls everything here and it controls all our foreign relations. It makes and breaks governments at will. No man and no body of men is more entrenched in power than the arrogant credit monopoly which operates the Federal Reserve Board and the Federal Reserve banks. These evil-doers have robbed this country of more than enough money to pay the national debt. What the Government has permitted the Federal Reserve Board to steal from the people should now be restored to the people." "Our people's money to the extent of $1,200,000,000 has within the last few months been shipped abroad to redeem Federal Reserve Notes and to pay other gambling debts of the traitorous Federal Reserve

Board and the Federal Reserve banks. The greater
part of our monetary stock has been shipped to
foreigners. Why should we promise to pay the debts
of foreigners to foreigners? Why should American
Farmers and wage earners add millions of foreigners
to the number of their dependents? Why should the
Federal Reserve Board and the Federal Reserve banks
be permitted to finance our competitors in all parts of
the world?" Rep. McFadden asked. "The Federal
Reserve Act should be repealed and the Federal
Reserve banks, having violated their charters, should
be liquidated immediately. Faithless government
officers who have violated their oaths should be
impeached and brought to trial", Rep. McFadden
concluded (Reference 1, contains an entire chapter on
Rep. McFadden's speech).

If the media is unbiased, independent and completely
thorough, why haven't they discussed the FED?
Currently, half the states have at least a grass roots
movement in action to abolish the FED, but there's no
press coverage. In July, 1968, the House Banking
Subcommittee reported that Rockefeller, through
Chase Manhattan Bank, controlled 5.9% of the stock in
CBS. Furthermore, the bank had gained interlocking

directorates with ABC. In 1974, Congress issued a report stating that the Chase Manhattan Bank's stake in CBS rose to 14.1% and NBC to 4.5% (through RCA, the parent company of NBC). The same report said that the Chase Manhattan Bank held stock in 28 broadcasting firms. After this report, the Chase Manhattan Bank obtained 6.7% of ABC, and today the percentage could be much greater. It only requires 5% ownership to significantly influence the media (Reference 14, P. 56-57). This is only one of 300 wealthy shareholders of the FED. It is believed other FED owners have similar holdings in the media. To control the media, FED bankers call in their loans if the media disagrees with them (Reference 25, P. 134-137). Rockefeller also controls the Council on Foreign Relations (CFR), the sole purpose of which is to aid in stimulating greater interest in foreign affairs and in a one world government. Nearly every major newscaster belongs to the Council on Foreign Relations. The Council on Foreign Relations controls many major newspapers and magazines. Additionally, major corporations owned by FED shareholders are the source of huge advertising revenues which surely would influence the media (Reference 14, P. 56-59). It can be no wonder why groups such as FED-UP(tm) receive minimal, if any, press attention. How do taxpayers stop financing those whose purpose it is to destroy us? First, expose their activity, then demand change. *The solution*: Currently all we do is exchange FED money (interest attached) for real U.S. money (interest-free) dollar for dollar as Kennedy tried to do. We should not be required to pay interest on our own currency. According to Benjamin Franklin, this was one of the primary reasons we fought the Revolutionary War. Today we are still fighting the same family of bankers (Reference 4, Reference 1, P. 211, 212). The U.S. Government can buy back the FED at any time for $450 million (per Congressional record). The U.S. Treasury could then collect all the profit on our money instead of the 300 original shareholders of the FED. The $4 trillion of U.S. debt could be exchanged dollar for dollar with U.S. non- interest bearing currency when the debt becomes due. There would be no inflation because there would be no additional currency in circulation. Personal income tax could be cut if we bought back the FED and therefore, the economy would expand. According to the Constitution, Congress is to control the creation of money, keeping the amount of inflation or deflation in check. If Congress isn't doing their job, they should be voted out of office. Unfortunately, voters can't vote the FED or its Chairman out of office. If the government has a deficit, we could handle it as Lincoln and Kennedy did. Print money and circulate it into the economy, but this time interest-free. Today the FED, through foreign banks, owns much of our debt and therefore controls us. The FED will cease to exist as taxpayers become informed and tell other taxpayers. The news media and Congress will have no choice but to meet the demands of grass roots America. (Reference 1, P. 17, 22)

America Deceived

By law (check the Congressional record), we can buy back the FED for the original investment of the FED's 300 shareholders, which is $450 million (Reference 1, P. 227, Reference 17, P. 36). If each taxpayer paid $25, we could buy back the FED and all the profit would flow into the U.S. Treasury. In other words, by Congress allowing the constitutionally illegal FED to continue, much of your taxes go to the shareholders of the FED and their bankers. Note: The people who enacted the FED started the IRS, within months of the FED's inception. The FED buys U.S. debt with money they printed from nothing, then charges the U.S. taxpayers interest. The government had to create income tax to pay the interest expense to the FED's shareholders, but the income tax was never legally passed (Reference 20 shows details, state-by-state why it was not legally passed). The FED is illegal, per Article 1, Section 8 of the United States Constitution. Not one state legally ratified the 16th Amendment making income tax legal. Currently, fewer and fewer Americans are being convicted for refusal to pay income taxes. In IRS jury trials, the jury, by law, must decide if the law is just. If taxpayers do not believe the law is just, the jury may declare the accused innocent. Judges are legally bound to inform juries of their right to determine the fairness of a law. Judges often do not disclose this information so they can control the court outcome. Luckily, more and more citizens are becoming informed. If one juror feels the law is unfair, they can find the defendant innocent (Reference 19). In Utah, the IRS quit prosecuting taxpayers because jurors verdict is not guilty. Please tell your friends and sit in the next jury. If we eliminate the FED and uphold the Constitution, we could balance the budget and cut personal income tax to almost nothing. In Congressional hearings on September 30, 1941, FED Chairman Eccles admitted that the FED creates new money from thin air (printing press), and loans it back to us at interest (Reference 17, P. 93). On June 6, 1960, FED President Mr. Allen admitted essentially the same thing (Reference 22, P. 164). If you or I did this we would go to jail. It is time to abolish the FED! Tell your friends the truth and win America back. We don't even need to buy back the FED. We only need to print money the way the Constitution requires, not the new proposed international money. We want to keep our sovereignty and print real U.S. money. Why has Congress allowed the FED to continue? If a Congressperson tries to abolish the FED, the banks fund the Congressperson's opponent in the next election (Reference 17, P. 35). The new Congressperson will obviously support the FED. When Congresspeople retire, political campaign funds are not taxed. Get elected and be a millionaire if you vote right. By the way, the profit of the FED is not taxed either (Reference 1, 9). Once America understands, and takes action, Congresspeople will then gladly abolish the FED. In 1992, Illinois Congressman Crane introduced a bill, co-sponsored by 40 other Congressman, to audit the FED. This is a step in the right direction. America is a great nation. As "We the People" become informed, the media and Congress will be forced to buy back the FED, balance the budget, significantly cut taxes, and stop allowing bribes to determine voting strategies. I have already heard from politicians who claim they will change their platform to include abolishing the FED if enough people become informed.

It is up to You to Inform the People

The FED hopes you will be passive and not act on this information. We believe in grass roots America – we are waking up America. Ultimately, the battle plan is to inform all Americans and demand change in the media and Congress. True Americans should run for office and throw out the politicians who allow this fraud to continue. Congress may refuse to deal with this issue. That's why each person needs to go to their local county/state government with the proper paperwork and ask them to abolish the FED. With the proper documents, they are legally obligated to do it. *We need leaders to begin this action. Will you help?* Consider this fact. Most of the given sources in this booklet show how the blood line of family bankers who own the FED funded both sides of all major wars. They created fake colonial money to destroy the Americans during the Revolutionary War and tried to finance both sides in the American Civil War. Abraham Lincoln refused and the South accepted. Many publications show that these bankers financed World War I, World War II, and the Russian Revolutionary War, which helped Napoleon, Lenin, and Hitler come to power. They financed both sides from money created from nothing and profited greatly. These same bankers created a number of American depressions to change the U.S. legislation and seize our wealth. Read the sources for details. This is why our forefathers wrote in the Constitution that only Congress can issue money - not private banks (Reference 18). More wars create more debt which means more profit to the bankers (Reference 1, 21). These bankers planned three world wars so people would welcome United Nations intervention to govern the world in peace, not war. (Reference 22 gives specific details on World War I and World War II, showing exactly how the bankers were responsible for the beginning and continuation of these wars for their profit). The banks have publicly announced they will force us to a cashless society by 1997. Furthermore, they plan to create a one world government through the United Nations headed by the FED, Trilaterals, and the Council on Foreign Relations (Reference 3). By the definition of treason, they have committed treason! This means you lose your rights under the Constitution and Bill of Rights. Does this sound far-fetched? Twenty-four U.S. Senators (two of them presidential candidates, Harkin & Tsongas) and 80 Representatives have signed a "Declaration of Interdependence." This Declaration, designed to make a one world government, is treason to the oath of office they took. The media remained silent. The FED announced publicly that their first objective was to get nationalism out of the American people's heads because patriotism to a country would not be of value in the future. The media makes us think the U.N. has all the answers, and to "think globally." Congress passed a law stopping certain individuals from being tried for this treason (Reference 6, Reference 1, P. 191-198). Why pass this law if no treason was committed? State Department document 7277 calls for the disarming of America, thus turning our sovereignty over to a one-world government. Again, the media is pushing to eliminate guns. Our forefathers believed that the right to bear arms would prevent a takeover of our government. History shows that before any government took over, they disarmed the citizens. Hitler did it, and before our Revolutionary War, King George told us to disarm – good thing we didn't! Under the Federal Reserve Bank Act, the bankers control our economy. The FED controls interest rates and the amount of money in the economy. These factors determine either economic prosperity or the lack thereof. Bankers are now pushing for a one world government and a cashless society. Why cashless? No cash means no money for drugs, no theft, and the ability to collect taxes on the underground economy. Anyone who wouldn't support a cashless society must be a drug dealer, thief, or tax evader, right? What a cashless society really means is the banks can now control you. Today you fear the IRS. In a cashless society, if you disagree with the bankers' political goals, you'll find your money gone via computer error. (For additional information on a cashless

society, read Reference 13, P. 174; Reference 3;
Reference 14, P. 9-12; Reference 15, P. 136; Reference
25, P. 216). If you could accurately predict future
interest rates, inflation and deflation, you would know
when to buy or sell stocks and make a bundle of money.
The FED has secret meetings (per Congressional
Record) to determine future interest rates and the
amount of money to be printed. The Securities
Exchange Commission (SEC) by law, stops insiders
from profiting by privileged information. Congressional
records prove that FED bankers routinely hold secret
meetings to profit by manipulating the stock market
via interest rates and the amount of money they
create. FED bankers also profit greatly from economic
disasters like the Depression (Reference 22, P. 56).
The bankers create inflation, sell their stocks before
the market crashes, then buy up stocks at cheaper
prices. Bankers admitted this to Congress. This
violates the law, yet Congress does not act because
these bankers are large political contributors
(Reference 17, P. 96-98; Reference 1, P. 162-163;
Reference 22, P. 114-170 & P. 136). Thomas Jefferson
predicted this scenario if we ever allowed a private
bank, like the FED, to create our currency (Reference

1, P. 247). FED Chairman Burns states "Killing can be made simply by knowing the next few months newspapers ahead of time." Congressman Patman said "The FED officials own more than 100 million dollars (of stocks) while making decisions influencing these stock prices..." (Reference 24, P. 123). History proves that banks profit from bankrupting a nation (Reference 22, P. 56). Congress consistently defeats balanced budget amendments. In the past 30 years, Congress has raised our taxes 56 times and balanced the budget only once. We need the sound banking system our forefathers wanted us to have. History proves that banking systems like the FED don't work. Major world powers have been destroyed over similar banking systems (Reference 1). If we don't change this system *now*, in five years the only thing our taxes will pay is the interest on the national debt. Section 7 of the Federal Reserve Act, passed December 23, 1913, states that much of the profit of the FED should flow into the U.S. Treasury. In 1959, new legislation allowed the FED to transfer bonds to commercial banks at no cost to the bank. Now the FED receives less interest income and less profit for the U.S. Treasury because the money is diverted to other banks through an accounting entry (Reference 17, P. 115-130). Congress and the IRS do not have access to the financial records of the FED. Every year Congress introduces legislation to audit the FED, and every year it is defeated. The FED banking system could easily be netting 100s of billions in profit each year. Through "creative accounting" profit can easily be reclassified as expense (Reference 14, P. 20, Reference 17, P. 239). Within the first few years, the shareholders of the FED received their initial investment back with no risk. All the income is tax-free, except for property tax, according to the Federal Reserve Act. When are the profits of the FED going to start flowing into the Treasury so that average Americans are no longer burdened with excessive, unnecessary taxes? Clearly, Congress cannot or will not control the FED. *It is time to abolish it!*

Three Ways To Abolish The Fed And Issue Money Per The US Constitution, Article 1, Section 8:

- Buy back the FED and have the U.S. Government collect all profits.
- Abolish the FED by printing real U.S. dollars as President Kennedy attempted (Executive Order 11.110, 1963) (Reference 4).
- Request your county/state to use their Constitutional powers to abolish the FED. This is the *best solution*.

Nearly half the states are attempting or considering this action (Reference 5). Congress has had 80 years to follow the Constitution, and has refused to abolish the illegal FED. The state/county effort is working faster than any other method. We need your support to start a local chapter of FED-UP(tm) Inc. and petition your county.

The wrong solution that has failed for 80 years: Congress and the media may want to require the FED to return the required profits into the U.S. Treasury (per the Federal Reserve Act, 1913). The problem is that with "creative accounting" techniques, profit can be easily masked as expense. The FED has expensed items illegally to lower profit (Reference 17). "We the People" have pushed the following states to pass or introduce legislation calling for an end to the FED: Arizona, Washington, Arkansas, Idaho, Oregon, Indiana, and Texas. We still need your signatures on petitions, even if you live in these states. Many other states are considering such action due to your petitions. These states and a few honest Congress people are powerless until all Americans become informed and demand change. Please pass out the petition. Once we demand change, the media will have to report the whole truth and not just push their own agenda. FED-UP(tm) challenges the media to expose the facts on prime time talk shows or news programs. By abolishing the FED, we would not pay interest on Federal Reserve Notes. Until it is abolished, the FED has a monopoly on profit on our currency and whether our money supply will be increased or decreased, inflation or depression. The banks are capable of controlling business by controlling who can or cannot obtain a loan. *We've done our part - now it is up to you to spread the word.* Please take the brochure (Cutting taxes $6,000 per family per year) to VFW, Moose/Elk Lodges, Bars, Union Halls, Churches, and Association groups. Make copies of the "single-page" brochure for everyone at work and ask your friends to do the same. Ask small business owners in your community to tell other business owners and spread the brochure and petition through the local Chamber of Commerce. CPAs should be interested in saving their clients taxes. Ask your CPA to mail the brochure and petition out to his/her clients. Upon receiving this petition, many presidents of large corporations made this brochure and petition available to all employees. Once people are informed, we can force a change. People will have more money to spend, the economy will be strong, and we can keep our Constitutional rights, liberties, and freedoms. Contact your library for the names and addresses of your local and federal Congress people. *Mail them an envelope without your name and address attached.* In the envelope, say "FED-UP(tm) Inc. Abolish the FED." Also enclose one teabag (Boston Tea Party). Ask your friends to do the same (give them the addresses). Politicians are aware of the "Teabag Protest." If you don't mail it in, they're going to believe that we're not organized or we just don't care. IF YOU DON'T DO

IT NO ONE ELSE WILL! Many Congress people want to make this change, but can't without the support of the people. Why Our Forefathers Fought The FED "Allow me to control the issue and the nation's money and I care not who makes its laws!" The above quote has long been attributed to the 18th century banker Amshell Rothschild (his blood line controls the FED). For if one unscrupulous group is allowed to print a nation's money - it can eventually use that money to gain control of the press AND the politicians - and thus gain control of making the nation's laws - and finally - control of the nation itself. (Reference 4) If you will take the time to read the reference material listed which has been researched by Professors of Universities, Congress people, etc., you will turn up information that might frighten you. For instance, in 1921 the stockholders of the Federal Reserve financed an organization called the "Council on Foreign Relations" (CFR). *Harper's magazine* called this the most powerful organization in the United States. Ninety percent of the people in the State Department and key positions in the Executive Branch are members of the CFR. The CFR publishes a magazine called "Foreign Affairs." Read it if you want to know what is going to happen in coming years. The CFR is in favor of a New World Order (Reference 3). Congressman Patman re-quoted Thomas Jefferson showing that our founding fathers knew this banking principle very well. "I believe that banking institutions are more dangerous to our liberties than standing armies...." "Already they have raised up a money aristocracy that has set the government at defiance. The issuing power (of money)," he said, "should be taken from the banks and restored to the people to whom it properly belongs." The American Revolution was a struggle to wrest control of wealth from the Bank of England and to restore the centers of power to the People where it "properly belongs." The Constitution is specific about the authority of the People, through their elected officials, to control the money, and thus, the affairs of their government. (Reference 5, P. 32). Ben Franklin said in his autobiography that the inability of the colonists to get the power to issue their own money permanently out of the hands of George III and the international bankers was [one of] the PRIME reason[s] for the Revolutionary War. (Quoted in Reference 4) Thomas Jefferson stated, "If the American people ever allow private banks to control the issue of currency, first by inflation, then by deflation, the banks and corporations that will grow up around them will deprive the people of all property until their children will wake up homeless on the continent their fathers conquered." (Reference 1, P. 247) Congressman Charles A. Lindbergh of Minnesota said: "This [Federal Reserve] Act establishes the most gigantic trust on Earth. When the President [Wilson] signs this bill, the invisible government of the Monetary Power will be legalized... the worst legislative crime of the ages, perpetuated by this banking and currency bill." (Reference 5, P. 33) Robert H. Hemphill (Credit Manager, Federal Reserve Bank in Atlanta): "We are completely dependent on the commercial banks. Someone has to borrow every dollar we have in circulation, cash, or credit. If the banks create ample synthetic money we are prosperous; if not, we starve. We are absolutely without a permanent money system. When one gets a complete grasp of the picture, the tragic absurdity of our hopeless position is almost incredible, but there it is. It [the banking problem] is the most important subject intelligent persons can investigate and reflect upon. It is so important that our present civilization may collapse unless it becomes widely understood and the defects are remedied very soon." (Reference 1, P. 247) Napoleon, a sympathizer for the international bankers, turned against them in the last years of his rule. He said: "When a government is dependent upon bankers for money, they and not the leaders of the government control the situation, since the hand that gives is above the hand that takes... Money has no motherland; financiers are without patriotism and without decency; their sole object is gain." (Reference 4) Congresspeople have referred to Federal Reserve Notes as "Fiat" (no-backing) money. (Reference 1, P. 128, 169) In 1879 the Supreme Court declared that the U.S. Government can legally issue United States Notes, debt and interest-free, just as Lincoln and Kennedy attempted. (Reference 1, P. 233) A bank that attempted to repossess property on the basis of default faced Judge Mahoney in a jury trial. Jerome Daly was found innocent. The bank could not foreclose on the property because it created the loan money from thin air, as many banks do. Use this as a precedent the next time any bank tries to foreclose on your house. (Reference 17, P. 82, 83 for court records) The FED violates Security & Exchange

Commission (SEC) rules. (Reference 17, P. 96-98) California 9th Circuit Court declared FED banks are private, not government. (Reference 17, P. 273) Mr. Marriner Eccles, who was Chairman of the board of Governors of the Federal Reserve System longer than any other man, testified before the Joint Economic Committee in August 1962. When Chairman Rep. Wright Patman asked whether it was not a fact that the Federal Reserve System has more power than either the Congress or the President, Eccles replied: "In the field of money and credit, yes." (Reference 1, P. 206) Dr. Hans F. Sennholz, Chairman of the Department of Economics at Grove City (PA) College stated: "The Federal Reserve System facilitates the government's own inflationary financing in "periods of emergency." It makes easy the inflationary financing of budget deficits and the inflationary refunding of government loans. It stabilizes the government bond market through inflationary methods and manipulates this market to the advantage of the government. It does all this by wrecking the purchasing power of the dollar; by subtly stealing from the people of this country what it thus provides for the government, through a process exactly on par with the coin clipping of ancient kings but much less visible." (Reference 1, P. 250, 251) Source: Banking Act of 1935, Hearings before a Subcommittee of the Banking and Currency Committee, U.S. Senate, 74th Congress, 1st Session, on S.1715, May 1935, pp 871-2. "The Federal Reserve System is in the wrong hands. No Constitutional republic can function when the government's money powers are in the hands of the financial oligarchy such as New York financiers. A Republican Senator, who preferred to remain unnamed, stated: "Congress is too much motivated by fears and anxieties concerning pressure groups and the "non-election." (Reference 1, P. 210) By controlling Congress, the FED has been able to control the nominating conventions of both political parties. In this way, it has been able to hand-pick the presidential nominees so that no matter which party wins, their nominee for President is under definite obligations to the FED... (Reference 1, P. 210; Reference 22) In 1975, the Rockefeller Foundation Report discussed the "Interdependence" of the countries of the world on each other. It stated we are one world and America shall become a nation-state under one government. They also say we must reach a zero state population growth. The Rockefeller

Foundation stated that they have in excess of 747 million dollars to achieve this with. (Reference 3) Congressman John R. Rarick states that the Council on Foreign Relations CFR) is dedicated to a one world government. The media remains conspicuously quiet. The CFR wants to convert the U.S. from a sovereign, constitutional republic into a servile member state of a one world dictatorship. On February 17, 1950, CFR member James Warburg (banker, and architect of the Federal Reserve System) stated before a Senate Foreign Relations Committee, "We shall have one world government whether or not you like it, by conquest or consent." Again, the media remained silent. In the April 1974 issue of the CFR journal, "Foreign Affairs", page 558, Richard Gardener states that the new world order "will be built... but an end run around national sovereignty, eroding it piece by piece, will accomplish much more than the old fashioned frontal assault." Congressman McDonald, Heinz and Tower stated that this is a conspiracy. Again, the media remained silent. (Reference 14, P. 17, 18, 32, 33). *The CFR wants to abolish the constitution (reference 14). We must stop them!!* In a letter to Thomas Jefferson, John Adams wrote: "All the perplexities, confusions, and distresses in America arise, not from defects in the Constitution or confederation, not from want of honor or virtue, as much as from downright ignorance of the nature of coin, credit, and circulation". British bankers have stated "Those that create and issue money and credit direct the policies of government and hold in their hands the destiny of the people". (Reference 1, P. 200-214) Adams, Jefferson, and Lincoln believed that banker capitalism was more dangerous to our liberties than standing armies. In a republic, banks would lend money but could not create or manufacture it. (Reference 1, P. 215) *Later, Jefferson used stronger language and denounced the institution as "one of the most deadly hostilities against the principles and form of our Constitution." Some have said that Jefferson did not favor a strong central bank. What he did not favor was the delivery of our monetary system into private hands to be run for private profit. (Reference 1, P. 230) President James A. Garfield said: "Whoever controls the money in any country is absolute master of industry [legislation] and commerce". (Reference 1, P. 247, Reference 4) Without the Federal Reserve System, there can be no continuing march towards socialism, and with it there can be no free economy.*

(Reference 1, P. 251) By controlling our own money, Thomas Jefferson expected that the government would incur no debt, as had occurred in the European system. (Reference 1, P. 243) European banks are like the FED. The FED system is the death of our Constitution. (Reference 1, P. 250) *the plan to reduce personal income tax by 75% and balance the budget by abolishing the fed can be proven by American history.*

The Facts

England lost the Revolutionary War.

England nearly destroyed the Colonies by creating fake Colonial money and hyper-inflation.

Rothschilds who control the Bank of England (Like our FED) said that by controlling the issue of money (printing it) you can control the government.

The authors of the Constitution understood private banks" control over governments. The Constitution gives only Congress the right to print money.

From the beginning of the United States to present there have been two ways to issue new currency: The first way is to have the government print the money, debt and interest- free, and circulate it through the economy for use as a medium of exchange.

There is no tax levied to pay interest on the currency in circulation because it is debt and interest-free. This is the system Lincoln used with his "greenbacks", a system Kennedy desired, and Jefferson demanded. The second method is: The Citizens allow the bank to print $500 billion in currency (cash). The bank pays for printing costs, ink, and paper. The Citizens do not charge the bank any interest for use of the $500 billion in printed currency. The bank uses the $500 billion cash to buy a $500 billion government bond which pays the bankers interest. The bank keeps some of the bonds and sells, for a fee (10%), some of the bonds to the public. The bank can buy back the bonds from the public simply by printing more money. The bankers can create inflation and depressions by manipulating the amount of currency in circulation. The FED operates exactly like this today. It also prints money (through the U.S. Treasury) and uses this printed money to buy loans from other banks. This money has created our inflation. We give the bank cash interest-free, then they charge us interest on our own currency. Take a look at our history in view of the two banking systems: Ben Franklin – *The Two Banking Systems*.

From the autobiography of Ben Franklin as reported by Gertrude Coogan in *Money Creators*: ...the inability of the colonists to get the power to issue their own money permanently out of the hands of George III and the international bankers was the PRIME reason for the Revolutionary War. (Reference 4). Ben Franklin answering a question about the booming economy of the young colonies: "That is simple. In the colonies we issue our own money. It is called Colonial Scrip. We issue it in proper proportions to the demands of trade and industry." (Colonial Scrip had no debt or interest attached.) (Reference 4)

Bank Of America

International bankers saw that interest-free scrip would keep America free of their influence, so by 1781 banker-backed Alexander Hamilton succeeded in starting the Bank of America. After a few years of "bank money", the prosperity of "Colonial Scrip" was gone. Benjamin Franklin said, "Conditions were so reversed that the era of prosperity had ended and a depression set in to such an extent that the streets of the Colonies were filled with the unemployed!" Bank money was like our FED money. It had debt and interest attached. By 1790 Hamilton and his bankers had created a privately owned central bank and converted the public debt (interest-free) into interest bearing bonds, payable to the bankers. When Hamilton's bank charter expired in 1811, the international bankers started the war of 1812. By 1816, another privately-owned U.S. bank was started with $35 million in assets - only $7 million of that was owned by the government. This bank lasted for 20 years. U.S. history shows that currency with debt and interest attached created a depression. (Reference 4)

Andrew Jackson - A Great President!

When the 1816 charter expired in 1836, Andrew Jackson vetoed its renewal. It was then that he made two famous statements: "The Bank is trying to kill me - but I will kill it!" Later he said "If the American people only understood the rank injustice of our money and banking system - there would be a revolution before morning..." (Reference 4)

Abraham Lincoln - Another Great President!

President Lincoln needed money to finance the Civil War, and the international bankers offered him loans at 24-36% interest. Lincoln balked at their demands because he didn't want to plunge the nation into such a huge debt. Lincoln approached Congress about passing a law to authorize the printing of U.S. Treasury Notes. Lincoln said "We gave the people of this Republic the greatest blessing they ever had - their own paper money to pay their debts..." Lincoln printed over 400 million "Greenbacks" (debt and interest-free) and paid the soldiers, U.S. government employees, and bought war supplies. The international bankers didn't like it and wanted Lincoln to borrow the money from them so that the American people would owe tremendous interest on the loan. Lincoln's solution made this seem ridiculous. (Reference 1, P. 46, 47; Reference 4)

Shortly after Lincoln's death, the government revoked the Greenback law which ended Lincoln's debt-free, interest-free money. A new national banking act was enacted and all money became interest bearing again. (Reference 4) The late Thomas A Edison explained the matter of issuing currency this way: "If our nation can issue a dollar bond (interest bearing) it can issue a dollar bill (interest-free). The element that makes the bond good makes a bill good also. The difference between the bond and the bill is that the bond lets money brokers collect twice the amount of the bond and an additional 20 percent, whereas the currency pays nobody but those who contribute directly in some useful way. It is absurd to say that our country can issue $30 million in bonds and not $30 million in currency. Both are promises to pay: But one promise fattens the usurers (interest collectors) and the other helps the people." (Reference 1, P. 46) The FED is owned largely by foreign banks that control our economy and Congress through the power of money and the media which they bought with profits generated with profits generated by artificial debt. If we can convert U.S. dollars that are debt and interest-free to interest bearing currency, we can change it back just as easily. Both the media and the banking system will probably claim that such a change will cause hyper-inflation. The answer however, can be found in history. Lincoln printed debt and interest-free Greenbacks (cash) to finance an entire war. With added production you can add currency without having hyper-inflation.

Lincoln proved it. John F. Kennedy - a President with vision! On June 4, 1964, President Kennedy issued Executive Order 11110. This Executive Order called for the issuance of new currency - the United States Note. At the time, $4,292,893 of this currency was put into circulation. This new currency was to be distributed through the U.S. Treasury and not the Federal Reserve System. Furthermore, it was to be issued debt and interest-free. Upon Kennedy's assassination, this currency was withdrawn from circulation, never to be issued again. The media remained silent on how Kennedy would have eliminated the debt and interest payments, and therefore eliminated the FED. Interest-free United States Notes do not result in hyper-inflation. By issuing United States Notes, interest-free, we have less interest expense, and less taxes. With less taxes people spend more and buy more. This result is added production, and therefore, you can add dollars without inflation. Either Rockefeller and his people will spend your tax money into the economy or you get to spend your own money by paying less taxes. The bankers want you to think you'll have mass inflation by changing the system. This is only true if you add dollars to the economy without added production. For example, look what happened in post World War I Germany. They merely printed money without increasing production. The result was hyper-inflation. Another example: In the entire economy, if you have only 10 loaves of bread and only $10, each loaf would sell for $1. If you print an extra $10, now you have $20 and the 10 loaves which would sell for $2 each. This is only true if we don't have added production. By cutting taxes, people will spend more and buy more bread. If we print more money and bake more bread, we have $50 and 50 loaves, so each loaf still sells for $1. As long as you monitor production with increased cash, inflation will not occur. Under the FED system, the price of bread has dramatically increased since 1913. If we cut taxes and you spend your money instead of the BANKERS spending it, you will have more bread, cars, and wealth than the bankers. *someone* will spend your money – it might as well be you! A FED-like banking system has destroyed other governments. In five years the only thing taxes will pay is the interest on the debt. Clearly, the FED must be abolished before we're demolished! Already laws are set up to have a dictatorship when we have the economic crisis (Federal Emergency

Management Act, or FEMA). Under the FED system, when a new dollar is issued, we pay taxes to pay for the dollar as the principal (debt) plus interest on the dollar. We pay for each new dollar twice, and who gets most of the money? The bankers, who control this money. Taxpayers should only pay taxes for the paper, ink, and printing costs of new money. Why should we give bankers the right to print money on a printing press, charge them no interest on this money, and then let them exchange their "free" money for a government bond that pays them interest? England never gave up on owning the United States. They are still silently fighting the same Revolutionary War. The Bank of England, through the Rothschilds, owns and controls the FED (Reference 22). We have been robbed of our wealth, and in five years we will be bankrupt if there is no change. The FED bankers will *legally own our nation; our houses, our cars, our businesses*, just as Thomas Jefferson predicted.

Specific Plan: How To Get Out Of Debt

U.S. history proves that issuing debt and interest-free currency allows our economy to prosper, as long as

Congress controls the amount of money created. You can add printed dollars into the economy as you add production, and there will be no inflation. With today's sophisticated computers, we can easily monitor the printing of money and inflation. Congress needs to buy back the FED and/or abolish it. Any government debt they own would be automatically eliminated. All remaining debt could be paid as needed with the same type of currency Kennedy issued (debt and interest-free United States Notes). United States Notes are backed by the full faith of the best government in the world - The United States of America. This is no different than the backing of today's Federal Reserve Notes. U.S. citizens collect only a small fraction of the interest income on Federal Bonds and Bills. Foreigners benefit from this interest, but we pay the tax so that they collect interest on our currency. This makes sense to bankers and Congress people who receive money from bankers and foreign lobbyists. As we pay less interest, government spending will decrease and so will taxes. Less taxes mean that people buy more goods and services and our economy expands. An expanded economy means more jobs and higher profits for businesses. More profit means increased state/federal business taxes. Businesses continue to pay taxes while personal taxes decrease. People will have more money to spend, will buy more, and therefore pay increased state sales tax. This allows the states to balance their budgets without raising real estate taxes. As history proves, we will prosper. For 80 years the FED has destroyed our economy. It will take years to undo this damage. Just as Congress appoints a Postal Service, we will have Congress appoint an agency to monitor inflation as we exchange our retiring government debt for debt and interest-free United States Notes (cash). We need to break up all Central Banks created by the FED and return to the Constitution of the United States. We have to return the power of the citizens' money back to the people.

Several Ways To Abolish The Fed:

- Inform all Americans of this report and collect signatures on the petition.
- Demand that Congress and the media support "We the People's" rights to uphold the Constitution and abolish the illegal FED.

- Write to your local newspaper, show them this report and ask them to keep freedom of the press alive, support the Constitution and abolish the FED. Freedom of the press should not be limited to those who own it.

- Write to CNN and other media. Tell them you want to see FED-UP(tm) on their programs.

- Ask your State/County Representatives to use their Constitutional powers to enforce your rights under the Constitution to have the FED abolished. Write to Reference 5 for detailed paperwork to be given to your local government.

- Call in on TV and radio talk shows and discuss why the FED should be abolished.

- Support businesses who distribute the petition and display the sign "FED-UP". If they don't, please ask them to.

- Ask candidates if they plan to introduce legislation to abolish the FED and uphold the Constitution which they are obligated to defend. Make candidates take a stand! Have the politician sign a contract with "We the People" enacting legislation to abolish the FED by a certain date or the politician must resign from office. The Democratic

Congress and President promised the people "no FED" before the election. Thirteen months later, they passed the FED.

- Display your bumper sticker to show support and inform people.

If 5,000 people distribute 2-3 brochures daily, we can inform half a million Americans monthly. Roughly 10% of these half a million people will make copies and inform others. Our goal is to inform 70 million adult Americans. Public opinion will soon be on our side. Once 10% of the population know, the other 90% will follow. Pray and ask God to return us to "One nation under God." It is our recommendation that you research the references listed, support all organizations that re trying to stop this fraud, and help us in our goal to get every American to sign this petition.

References

(1) "The Federal Reserve Bank", by H.S. Kenan, published by The Noontide Press

(2) National Committee to Repeal the Federal Reserve Act, P.O. Box 156, Westmont, IL 60559

(3) "The New World Order,Saving America", P.O. Box 1205, Middleburg, FL 32050-1205

(4) "Bulletin", February 1989 & November 1991 issues, P.O. Box 986, Ft. Collins, CO 80522 (Newsletter; $3 each)

(5) "The Most Secret Science", Betsy Ross Press, P.O. Box 986, Ft. Collins, CO 80522 (Book)States attempt to abolish the FED. $12.00

(6) "Insider Report", P.O. Box 84903, Phoenix, AZ 85071

(7) "Phoenix Journal Express", P.O. Box 986, Tehachap, CA 93581

(8) $16 trillion in government and private debt, much of which the FED printed and collected interest on (Ref. 3)

(9) Northpoint Tactical Team, P.O. Box 129, Topton, NC 28781

(10)Christian Defense League, Box 449, Arabi, LA 70023

(11)"Bulletin", June 1992 issue, P.O. Box 986, Ft. Collins, CO 80522 (Newsletter; $3 each)

(12)"Savings and Loan Unethical Bailout" by Rev. Casimir F. Gierut

(13)"Dark Secrets of the New Age" by Texe Marrs

(14)"En Route to Global Occupation" by Gary H. Kah

(15)"One World" by John Amkerberg & John Weldon

(16)"The Spotlight", Liberty Lobby, 300 Independence Ave. S.E., Washington, D.C. 20003 (Newspaper)

(17)"Repeal the Federal Reserve Banks" by Rev. Casimir Frank Gierut

(18)The Constitution of the United States

(19)"Walls in Our Minds" by M.J. Red Beckman, Common Sense Press, P.O. Box 1544, Billings, MT 59103. A must read book - $2.50

(20)"The Law That Never Was" Volume I, Bill Benson & M.J. Red Beckman, P.O. Box 1544, Billings, MT 59103 or write to Bill Benson, P.O. Box 550, South Holland, IL 60473. Proof that the 16th Amendment (income tax)was never properly ratified.

(21)"New World Order: The Ancient Plan of Secret Societies" by William T. Still

(22)"The Secrets of the Federal Reserve" by Mullins

(23)"The Social Security & Pension Conspiracy" by Metz

(24)"The History of the Federal Reserve. How to Replace It or How to Reform It" by Metz - for references 23 & 24 write to Howard Metz, P.O. Box 341, Malverne, LI 11565

(25)"The New World Order" by Pat Robertson. On page 131 he states that we must abolish the FED.

(26)"Operation Vampire Killer 2000", highly recommended book. $6.00 ($8.00 for 2)from ACLA, P.O. Box 8712, Phoenix, AZ 85066 This is a must read book with quotes from well-known people. This book proves conspiracy. Your local police needs to read this book so they will protect you – not become United Nations Agents against you. This book will stop the New World Order plan to take over the U.S.A. "America Betrayed", Center For Action, 652 N. Glenview, Nesa, AZ 85213

For references 1, 12, and 17, contact The National Committee to Repeal the Federal Reserve Act

(Reference 2) *Media Blacks Out The Facts* Here's one terrific example. John Swinton, the former Chief of Staff for the New York Times, was one of New York's best loved newspapermen. Called by his peers "The Dean of his Profession", John was asked in 1953 to give a toast before the New York Press Club, and in so doing, made a monumentally important and revealing statement. He is quoted as follows: "There is no such thing, at this date of the world's history, in America, as an independent press. You know it and I know it. There is not one of you who dares to write your honest opinions, and if you did, you know beforehand that it would never appear in print. I am paid weekly for keeping my honest opinion out of the paper I am connected with. Others of you are paid similar weekly salaries for similar things, and any of you who would be so foolish as to write honest opinions would be out on the streets looking for another job. If I allowed my honest opinions to appear in one issue of my paper, before twenty-four hours my occupation would be gone. The business of the journalists is to destroy the truth; to lie outright; to pervert; to vilify; to fawn at the feet of mammon, and to sell his country and his race for his daily bread. You know it and I know it, and what folly is this toasting an independent press? We are the tools and vassals of rich men behind the scenes. We are the jumping jacks, they pull the strings and we dance. Our talents, our possibilities, and our lives are all the property of other men. We are intellectual prostitutes." Richard M. Cohan, Senior Producer of CBS political news said: "We are going to impose our agenda on the coverage by dealing with issues and subjects that we choose to deal with." Richard Salant, former President of CBS News stated: "Our job is to give people not what they want, but what we decide they ought to have." And what is "their" agenda? What do they believe we, the American people, – the common herd, "...ought to have?" Here is the answer: Norman Thomas – For many years the U.S. Socialist Presidential candidate proclaimed: "The

American people will never knowingly adopt Socialism. But under the name of "liberalism" they will adopt every fragment of the socialist program, until one day America will be a Socialist nation, without knowing what happened." Herman Dismore, foreign editor of the New York Times from 1950 to 1960: "The New York Times is deliberately pitched to the liberal (socialist) point of view." Walter Cronkite: "News reporters are certainly liberal (socialists) and left of center." Barbara Walters: "The news media in general are liberals (socialists)." Reference for everything above - Operation Vampire Killer, P.O. Box 8712, Phoenix, AZ 85066 The world, finally including even the balky American public, is "being rapidly educated into overcoming limited patriotism" and accepting "United Nations solutions to common global problems," said Henry Kissinger. Bilderberg participants expressed satisfaction with progress toward world government on two fronts:

Establishing a UN tax to not only finance new global programs, but to condition "citizens of the world" to paying tribute.

Conditioning the public –again, especially "those stubborn Americans"– to accept the idea of a UN army that could, by force, impose its will on the internal affairs of any nation. "Today, Americans would be outraged if UN forces entered Los Angeles to restore order; tomorrow, they will be grateful," Kissinger said (of the 1992 Los Angeles riot). Kissinger reported on a shocking speech made by UN Secretary General Boutros Ghali to the American Association of Newspaper Publishers at UN headquarters in New York in early May. The publishers' newspapers covered up the story. The UN Security Council must have a permanent force that can be deployed anywhere in the world, instantly, to "protect the peace" and "ensure human rights" the secretary-general told the newspaper publishers.

UN to Invade US

This force must be allowed to intervene "at the local and community levels," the UN leader told the American publishers. What is "especially gratifying," Kissinger said, "is that the publishers showed no reservations about the prospects of UN forces landing in the United States and imposing the UN's will." Reference - The Spotlight, June 8, 1992, page 10.

Liberty Lobby, 300 Independence Ave. S.E., Washington, D.C. 20003 (Newspaper)

Summary Of Quick Facts

Various dates and proofs that the Bankers created panic to push Congress to pass laws favoring bankers... Reference 22

President Wilson received $85,000 bribe from bankers... Reference 22, pages 25-26

How England, through the Bankers, controls our Congress... Reference 22, pages 47-48

Rockefeller is connected to President Carter... Reference 22, page 171; Reference 25, page 103

How George Bush is directly connected to the FED bank... Reference 22, page 49

President Hoover and President Roosevelt were international Bankers... Reference 22, pages 69-71 and pages 157-159

President Nixon was hired by Rockefeller's law firm to become President... Reference 25, pages 100-101

FED owner's manual to destroy and control U.S. citizens... Reference 22, pages 55-56

Proof Bankers claim they control the government...
Reference 22, page 59

Proof the FED knowingly created the Great Depression
for their gain... Reference 22, pages 137-170

FED bankers are directly linked to the New World
Order and the United Nations. New World Order was
discussed by George Bush, Rockefeller, Adolph Hitler,
and Jimmy Carter... Reference 25, pages 5-7

The Great Seal on back of the FED $1 bill, below
pyramid, the NOVUS ORDO SECLORUM means "New
World of the Ages" or --->> New World Order...
Reference 25, page 35

How the Banker's tax-exempt organizations fund
activities to destroy America's freedom by attacking
our Constitution and way of life... Reference 25, pages
138-159; Reference 14 (throughout whole book)

Senator Barry Goldwater warned of economic powers
capable of bypassing or controlling the political
powers. Bank induced depression is possible in the
future to force political change... Reference 25, 131

Rockefeller's money was used to seize control of
America's teaching and training of students by
rewriting history and textbooks. Rockefeller has also

funded the National Education Association (NEA)... Reference 14, page 61

Gary Kah, high-ranking government liaison having first-hand knowledge of the New World Order exposes the truth. Read his book and En Route To Global Occupation... Reference 14

Quick Facts From Tom Schauf

First, we must uphold the Constitution. Please call the Hotline (217-854-7504) weekly for new information. When a state considers a Constitutional Convention, concerned Americans call the Hotline and it gives us the names and telephone numbers of the legislators involved. It tells us exactly what to say, and to whom. The Hotline helps us to fight and win! Secondly, we must change the opinions of the masses with information. The brochure has been a big help, and once 10% of the population agrees to abolish the FED, the rest will follow. It is obvious the media (radio and newspapers) have lied about the FED and the efforts of FED-UP(tm) to educate people with the truth. This will not stop us - we will persist! Decide for yourself if you want to win America back. If 10,000 patriotic

Americans each distribute 1,000 brochures, 10 million Americans will become informed. It would be almost impossible to stop people from talking about abolishing the FED if that many Americans were informed. Another way you can participate is to put a bumper sticker on your car. Over 1,000 people every month will see that bumper sticker about abolishing the FED. If you think our goal is impossible, remember this; only 3% of Americans supported the Revolutionary War, and we won that war. We can win this war too, but only with your help. IN CLOSING For the secret owners of the FED to control the volume of money and become our absolute masters, they had to get the Gold away from our grandparents. This was accomplished in 1933 with the threats of fines and imprisonments by their President Franklin D. Roosevelt with aide Harry Hopkins, who said... "Elect, elect, elect, tax, tax, tax, spend, spend, spend, for the people are too damned stupid to understand". By the way, Roosevelt was an international Banker. See Fool's Gold is Green by Winston Smith.

The FED is Slowly Destroying America

Our government never had a chance...with political corruption ravaging its Constitution. The "real facts" don't lie...and neither do government documents...Congressional Record, Congressman Wright Patman, A Primer On Money prepared by the Sub-committee on Domestic Finance, House of Representatives, Committee on Banking and Currency - 88th Congress, 2nd session, August 4th, 1964 and December 23, 1913, page 1464 & 1478. Congressional Record, Congressman Louis McFadden, June 10, 1932, House of Representatives, pages 12604-12605 Congressional Record, 98th Congress, 1st session, February 3, 1983, Congressman Ron Paul Congressional Record, Committee on Banking and Currency, House of Representatives, 77th Congress, 1st session, Tuesday, September 30, 1941, pages 1342-1345 *there are many more congressional testimonials is there bias in the media regarding the fed? During the TV presidential debates, Clinton was asked should there be restrictions on the FED? The next day, major newspapers said they covered the whole presidential debate text, but many newspapers eliminated this one question. Check your library! The Revolutionary War* was fought and the Constitution was written to prevent other nations and private banks from issuing (printing) money and controlling our currency. In 1913, members of Congress committed treason and violated their oath of office to defend the Constitution against all enemies foreign and domestic by voting in the Federal Reserve Bank. For the New World Order to create a one world government, they must control a central bank, eliminate the Constitution, end Christian values, disarm America, and control the media. The Council on Foreign Relations has openly said they will take us over in favor of a one world government. The American people must be warned or we may lose our freedom forever. If we do not demand our rights and uphold the Constitution, the CFR and bankers will continue their march toward socialism. If we allow them to continue, they will abolish our rights and put an end to our present government. I urge all Americans to distribute the "main" FED-UP brochure ("saving $6000 in taxes per year, per person & balancing the budget) and collect signatures on the petition (see order form in the main brochure). Then all informed Americans can take action and hold their politicians accountable. The bankers control the media, but cannot stop patriotic Americans from using copy machines to distribute information and inform America. Once informed, people will demand an explanation why Congress allowed this fraud as the media appeared to be independent and investigative, but remained silent on this important issue. The ones who scream the loudest to keep the Federal Reserve Bank probably profit the most.

About the Author: Thomas D. Schauf, CPA, is a national speaker to Certified Public Accountants and business leaders. Mr. Schauf's expertise includes banking, the economy, business appraisals, mergers, and acquisitions.

APPENDIX 5

U.S. *"War On Terror" Has Increased Terrorism*

by George Washington,[31] October 2013

The National Consortium for the Study of Terrorism and Responses to Terrorism (START) Global Terrorism Database – part of a joint government-university program on terrorism - is hosted at the University of Maryland. START is the most comprehensive open source terrorism database, which can be viewed by journalists and civilians lacking national security clearance. A quick review of charts from the START database show that terrorism has increased in the last 9 years since the U.S. started its "war on terror". This chart shows the **number of terror attacks** conducted in Iraq, Afghanistan, the

---

[31] https://www.zerohedge.com/contributed/2013-10-22/us-"war-terror"-has-increased-terrorism

Middle   East,   Asia,   Africa,   and   the   world, respectively.[32]

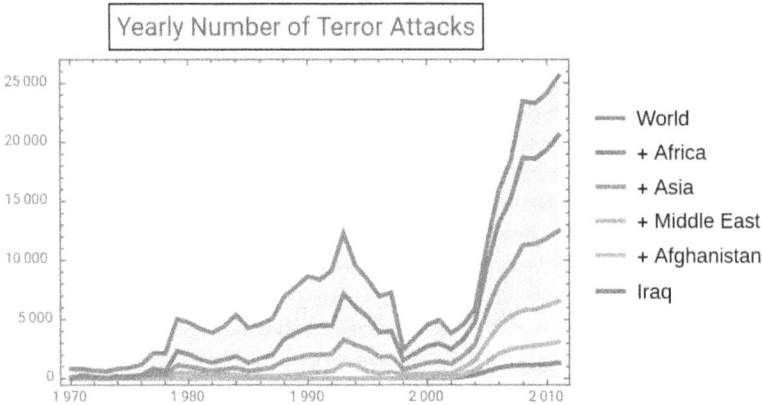

Yearly Number of Terror Attacks

This graph shows the number of terror attacks from the years 1970 through 2011. Indeed, global terrorism had been falling from 1992 until 2004 ... but has been skyrocketing since 2004. When a plot legend starts with a + sign, this indicates a cumulative value. Hence, the yellow line displays the number of terror attacks in both Iraq and Afghanistan. Upon including all

[32] Of course, one would prefer a chart displaying the number of casualties. However, this information is much harder to obtain, and subject to personal preconceptions.

continents in the world, the last cumulative continent would therefore coincide with the "world" graphic.

Clearly, since the "war on terror" began in 1970, there was a steady increase until 1993, followed by a relative dip in 1998 (at a triple level compared to that in 1970). Ever since it has been exploding to unprecedented numbers.

Our Wars In the Middle East Have Created More Terrorists

Security experts – including both conservatives and liberals – agree that waging war in the Middle East weakens national security and increases terrorism.[33] Ooops.

---

33 http://www.foreignpolicy.com/articles/2010/10/18/
it_s_the_occupation_stupid;
http://www.washingtonpost.com/wp-
dyn/content/article/2006/09/23/AR2006092301130.html
http://www.counterpunch.org/feingold09292005.html
http://www.fromthewilderness.com/free/ww3/100102_against
_war.html
http://www.rand.org/news/press/2008/07/29/
http://www.salon.com/news/opinion/glenn_greenwald/2010/1
0/12/terrorism
http://www.guardian.co.uk/world/2012/jul/30/syria-foreign-
jihadists-aleppo-al-qaida

Killing innocent civilians is one of the main things which
increases terrorism. As one of the top counter-
terrorism experts (the former number 2 counter-
terrorism expert at the State Department) told me,
starting wars against states which do not pose an
imminent threat to America's national security
increases the threat of terrorism because:

One of the principal causes of terrorism is injuries to
people and families. The Iraq war wasn't even fought
to combat terrorism. And Al Qaeda wasn't even in Iraq
until the U.S. invaded that country. And top CIA
officers say that drone strikes increase terrorism.[34]

Furthermore, James K. Feldman – former professor of
decision analysis and economics at the Air Force
Institute of Technology and the School of Advanced
Airpower Studies – and other experts say that foreign
occupation is the main cause of terrorism. University
of Chicago professor Robert A. Pape – who specializes
in international security affairs – points out:

Extensive research into the causes of suicide
terrorism proves Islam isn't to blame — the root of

---

34 http://www.youtube.com/watch?v=odXIutYn-lQ

the problem is foreign military occupations. (...) Each
month, there are more suicide terrorists trying to kill
Americans and their allies in Afghanistan, Iraq, and
other Muslim countries than in all the years before
2001 combined.

New research provides strong evidence that suicide
terrorism such as that of 9/11 is particularly sensitive
to foreign military occupation, and not Islamic
fundamentalism or any ideology independent of this
crucial circumstance. Although this pattern began to
emerge in the 1980s and 1990s, a wealth of new data
presents a powerful picture. More than 95 percent of
all suicide attacks are in response to foreign
occupation, according to extensive research [co-
authored by James K. Feldman - former professor of
decision analysis and economics at the Air Force
Institute of Technology and the School of Advanced
Airpower Studies] that we conducted at the
University of Chicago's Project on Security and
Terrorism, where we examined every one of the over
2,200 suicide attacks across the world from 1980 to
the present day. As the United States has occupied
Afghanistan and Iraq, which have a combined
population of about 60 million, total suicide attacks

worldwide have risen dramatically — from about 300 from 1980 to 2003, to 1,800 from 2004 to 2009. Further, over 90 percent of suicide attacks worldwide are now anti-American. The vast majority of suicide terrorists hail from the local region threatened by foreign troops, which is why 90 percent of suicide attackers in Afghanistan are Afghans. Israelis have their own narrative about terrorism, which holds that Arab fanatics seek to destroy the Jewish state because of what it is, not what it does. But since Israel withdrew its army from Lebanon in May 2000, there has not been a single Lebanese suicide attack. Similarly, since Israel withdrew from Gaza and large parts of the West Bank, Palestinian suicide attacks are down over 90 percent.

The first step is recognizing that occupations in the Muslim world don't make Americans any safer — in fact, they are at the heart of the problem.

Our Program of Torture Created Terrorists
In addition, torture creates new terrorists:

A top counter-terrorism expert says torture increases the risk of terrorism.[35]

One of the top military interrogators said that torture by Americans of innocent Iraqis is the main reason that foreign fighters started fighting against Americans in Iraq in the first place.[36] Former counter-terrorism czar Richard A. Clarke says that America's indefinite detention without trial and abuse of prisoners is a leading Al Qaeda recruiting tool. A former FBI interrogator — who interrogated Al Qaeda suspects — says categorically that torture actually turns people into terrorists. A 30-year veteran of CIA's operations directorate who rose to the most senior managerial ranks, says: "Torture creates more terrorists and fosters more acts of terror than it could possibly neutralize."

A former US Air Force interrogator said that torture just creates more terrorists

---

35 http://www.washingtonsblog.com/2009/05/terrorism-expert-keeping-detainees-in.html
36 http://georgewashington2.blogspot.com/2009/05/one-of-militarys-top-interrogators-says.html

A former U.S. interrogator and counterintelligence agent, and Afghanistan veteran said, "Torture puts our troops in danger, torture makes our troops less safe, torture creates terrorists. It's used so widely as a propaganda tool now in Afghanistan. All too often, detainees have pamphlets on them, depicting what happened at Guantanamo."

The Senate Armed Services Committee unanimously stated:

"The administration's policies concerning [torture] and the resulting controversies ... strengthened the hand of our enemies."

Two professors of political science have demonstrated that torture increases, rather than decreases, terrorism

General Petraeus said that torture hurts our national security

And the reporter who broke Iran-Contra and other stories says that torture actually helped Al Qaeda, by giving false leads to the U.S. which diverted its military, intelligence and economic resources into wild goose chases

So the widespread program of torture under the Bush administration didn't help.

Nice Job Creating More Terrorists, You Morons …
Additionally – in the name of fighting our enemies – the U.S. has directly been supporting Al Qaeda and other terrorist groups for the last decade. See this, this, this, this and this.

Why Have We Given Up Our Rights If the Government Can't Keep Us Safe?
We have given up the fundamental rights which make us American. The government insisted that – if we gave up our liberties – it would keep us safe. It has failed to do so, and has instead squandered our national treasure, our resources and our troops on efforts which have only increased the risk of terrorism.

Wasted Defense Spending
A large amount of the homeland security spending has been wasted … producing "a bunch of crap". For example, spending money on zombie apocalypse training or other silly programs is a bad investment which led to a false sense of security. Spending defense money on a workshop called "Did Jesus die for Klingons too?" and DOD-run microbreweries is probably not helping stop terrorist attacks. Moreover, using homeland security resources to spy on average Americans or crack down on peaceful protesters or government

critics distracts from getting the actual bad guys. At the same time, both the Bush and Obama administrations have slashed funding for programs which would actually help prevent terror attacks. Heck of a job, guys ...

The Real Agenda

Regime change was planned throughout the Middle East and North Africa were planned 20 years ago ... long before 9/11. As just one example, U.S. Secretary of Defense Chuck Hagel, 4-Star General (and CENTCOM commander with responsibility for Iraq) John Abizaid, key war architect John Bolton, a high-level National Security Council officer, President George W. Bush, Bush speech writer David Frum, Senator John McCain, Fed boss Alan Greenspan and Sarah Palin all say that the Iraq war was about oil. Documents from Britain show the same thing. Much of the war on terror is really a fight for natural gas. Or to force the last few hold-outs into dollars and private central banking. Senior government officials have described terrorist attacks as a "small price to pay for being a superpower". And while politicians talk about ending the war on terror, endless war is a feature – not a bug – of our foreign policy. Whatever the real agenda one thing is clear ... In the same way that NSA spying isn't about preventing terrorism,[37] the war on terror is cover for other shenanigans.

---

37 http://www.washingtonsblog.com/2013/10/spies-can-now-for-the-first-time-monitor-everything-about-us-and-they-can-do-so-with-a-few-clicks-of-a-mouse-and-to-placate-the-lawyers-a-drop-down-menu-of-justifications.html
http://www.washingtonsblog.com/2013/10/nsa-spying-makes-the-internet-and-computers-less-safe.html
http://www.washingtonsblog.com/2013/10/nsa-busted-conducting-industrial-espionage-in-france-mexico-brazil-and-other-countries.html
http://www.washingtonsblog.com/2013/10/nsa-spying-did-not-result-in-one-stopped-terrorist-plot-and-the-government-actually-did-spy-on-the-bad-guys-before-911.html

APPENDIX 6

List of American "Depressions"

Here follow some lists of American "depressions", as taken from Wikipedia.[38] The explanation of these depressions is very, very colorful. Too colorful. In reality, all these seemingly different explanations only divert the attention from what really was going on in the USA: A bunch of ordinary thieves organized the same financial scam over and over again. They used their banks to progressively strip the American people off their property.

---

38 https://en.wikipedia.org/wiki/
    List_of_recessions_in_the_United_States.

The panic of 1785 ended the business boom that followed the American Revolution. The causes of the crisis lay in the overexpansion and debts incurred after the victory at Yorktown, a postwar deflation, competition in the manufacturing sector from Britain, and lack of adequate credit and a sound currency. The downturn was exacerbated by the absence of any significant interstate trade. Other factors were the British refusal to conclude a commercial treaty. The panic among business and propertied groups led to the demand for a stronger federal government.

The 1789 loss of confidence in copper coins due to debasement and counterfeiting led to commercial freeze up that halted the economy of several northern States and was not alleviated until the introduction of new paper money to restore confidence. During that same time the Panic of 1792 took place. Its causes included the extension of credit and excessive speculation. The panic that was largely solved by providing banks the necessary funds to make open market purchases.

Just as a land speculation bubble was bursting,
deflation from the Bank of England (which was
facing insolvency because of the cost of Great
Britain's involvement in the French Revolutionary
Wars) crossed to North America and disrupted
commercial and real estate markets in the United
States and the Caribbean, and caused **the major
1796 financial panic**. Prosperity continued in the
south, but economic activity was stagnant in the
north for three years. The young United States
engaged in the Quasi-War with France.

A boom of war-time activity led to a decline after
the Peace of Amiens ended the war between the
United Kingdom and France. **Commodity prices fell
dramatically in 1802**. Trade was disrupted by
pirates, leading to the First Barbary War.

1807   The Embargo Act of 1807 was passed by
the United States Congress under President
Thomas Jefferson as tensions increased with the
United Kingdom. Along with trade restrictions
imposed by the British, shipping-related industries
were hard hit. The Federalists fought the embargo
and allowed smuggling to take place in New England.

Trade volumes, commodity prices and securities prices all began to fall. Macon's Bill Number 2 ended the embargoes in May 1810, and a recovery started.

The United States entered a brief recession at the beginning of 1812. The decline was brief primarily because the United States soon increased production to fight the War of 1812, which began June 18, 1812.

Shortly after the war ended on March 23, 1815, the United States entered a period of financial panic as bank notes rapidly depreciated because of inflation following the war. The 1815 panic was followed by several years of mild depression, and then a major financial crisis – the Panic of 1819, which featured widespread foreclosures, bank failures, unemployment, a collapse in real estate prices, and a slump in agriculture and manufacturing.

After only a mild recovery following the lengthy 1815–21 depression, **commodity prices hit a peak**

in March 1822 and began to fall. Many businesses failed, unemployment rose and an increase in imports worsened the trade balance

1825   The Panic of 1825, a stock crash following a bubble of speculative investments in Latin America led to a decline in business activity in the United States and England. The recession coincided with a major panic, the date of which may be more easily determined than general cycle changes associated with other recessions.

1828   In 1826, England forbade the United States to trade with English colonies, and in 1827, the United States adopted a counter-prohibition. Trade declined, just as credit became tight for manufacturers in New England.

1833   The United States' economy declined moderately in 1833–34. News accounts of the time confirm the slowdown. The subsequent expansion was driven by land speculation.

The earliest recessions for which there is the most certainty are those that coincide with major financial crises. In 1791, Congress chartered the First Bank of the United States to handle the country's financial needs. The bank had some functions of a modern central bank, although it was responsible for only 20% of the young country's currency. In 1811 the bank's charter lapsed, but it was replaced by the Second Bank of the United States, which lasted from 1816–36. The above table, taken from the previously quoted Wikipedia site, shows that most of the recessions are due to wars (the financial crises included). *This characteristic can be generalized to all recessions in general: there is always a war involved, started by a number of highly influential and immoral people.* The wars need not be of the 19th century classical kind: two opposed armies in open field, beautifully arranged, first row kneeled, following the orders "fire", "charge", and so forth. They can be quite different wars, e.g., due to co-signing an immoral political alliance.

APPENDIX 7
Free Banking Era to the Great Depression

Compared to today, the era from 1834 to the Great Depression was characterized by relatively severe and more frequent banking panics and recessions. In the 1830s, U.S. President Andrew Jackson fought to end the Second Bank of the United States, because he knew it was directed by a sordid mafia. The large majority of American Presidential executions were indeed ordered by banker mafias.[39] Following the Bank War, the

---

39 People sometimes associate the word "mafia" with Al Capone and his Italian fellows. In that sense it is obviously nonsensical to attribute JFK's murder to the mafia, even though it was the Italian mafia who delivered the decisive head shot (James Files' lead-filled bullet from the Grassy Knoll). In military executions one always has to differentiate between the peloton members, usually reluctant and innocent soldiers on one hand , and the judge who issued the execution order on the other. In the JFK murder, the CIA (George W.H. Bush) and the Italian mob only played the peloton role. The responsible judge was EZ, who

Second Bank lost its charter in 1836. From 1837 to 1862, there was no national presence in banking, but still plenty of state and even local regulation, such as laws against branch banking which prevented diversification. In 1863, in response to financing pressures of the Civil War, Congress passed the National Banking Act, creating nationally chartered banks.

---

obviously did not like JFK's financial Executive Order 11,110, as it would not fail to ruin their dirty FED business.

1836: UE dip=-32.8%

A sharp downturn in the American economy was caused by bank failures, lack of confidence in the paper currency, tightening of English Credit, crop failures and Jacksonian policy. Over 600 banks failed in this period. In the South, the cotton market completely collapsed.

1840: UE dip=-34.3%

This was one of the longest and deepest depressions of the 19th century. It was a period of pronounced deflation and massive default on debt. The Cleveland Trust Company Index showed the economy spent 68 months below its trend and only 9 months above it. The Index declined 34.3% during this depression.

1845: UE dip=-5.9%

This recession was so mild that it was but a slowdown in the growth cycle.

1847: UE dip=-19.7%

The Cleveland Trust Company Index declined 19.7% during 1847 and 1848. It is associated with a financial crisis in Great Britain.

1853: UE dip=-18.4%

Interest rates rose in this period, contributing to a decrease in railroad investment. Security prices fell during this period. With the exception of falling business investment there is little evidence of contraction in this period.

1857: UE dip=-23.1%

Failure of the Ohio Life Insurance and Trust Company burst a European speculative bubble in United States' railroads and caused a loss of confidence in American banks. Over 5,000 businesses failed within the first year of the Panic, and unemployment was accompanied by protest meetings in urban areas.

1860: UE dip=-14.5%

There was a recession before the American Civil War, which began April 12, 1861. Zarnowitz says the data generally show a contraction occurred in this period, but it was quite mild. A financial panic was narrowly averted in 1860 by the first use of clearing house certificates between banks.

1865: UE dip=−23.8%

The American Civil War ended in April 1865, and the country entered a lengthy period of general deflation that lasted until 1896. The United States occasionally experienced periods of recession during the Reconstruction era. Production increased in the years following the Civil War, but the country still had financial difficulties.

1869: UE dip=−9.7%

A few years after the Civil War, a short recession occurred. It was unusual since it came amid a period when railroad investment was greatly accelerating, even producing the First Transcontinental Railroad. The railroads built in this period opened up the interior of the country, giving birth to the Farmers' movement. The recession may be explained partly by ongoing financial difficulties following the war, which discouraged businesses from building up inventories. Several months into the recession, there was a major financial panic.

1873: UE dip=-30%

Economic problems in Europe prompted the failure of Jay Cooke & Company, the largest bank in the United States, which burst the post-Civil War speculative bubble. The Coinage Act of 1873 also contributed by immediately depressing the price of silver, which hurt North American mining interests. The deflation and wage cuts of the era led to labor turmoil, such as the Great Railroad Strike of 1877. In 1879, the United States returned to the gold standard with the Specie Payment Resumption Act. This is the longest period of economic contraction recognized by the NBER. The Long Depression is sometimes held to be the entire period from 1873-96.

1882: UE dip=-32.8%

This recession was more of a price depression than a production depression. From 1879 to 1882, there had been a boom in railroad construction which came to an end, resulting in a decline in both railroad construction and in related industries, particularly iron and steel.

1887: UE dip=-14.6%

Investments in railroads and buildings weakened during this period. This slowdown was so mild that it is not always considered a recession. Contemporary accounts apparently indicate it was considered a slight recession.

1890: UE dip=-22.1%

Although shorter than the recession in 1887-88 and still modest, a slowdown in 1890-91 was somewhat more pronounced than the preceding recession. International monetary disturbances are blamed for this recession, such as the Panic of 1890 in the United Kingdom.

1893: UE dip=-37.3%

Failure of the United States Reading Railroad and withdrawal of European investment led to a stock market and banking collapse. Profits, investment and income all fell, leading to political instability.

1896: UE dip=-25.2%

The period of 1893-97 is seen as a generally depressed cycle that had a short spurt of growth in the middle, following the Panic of 1893. Production shrank and deflation reigned.

1899: UE dip=-15.5%
This was a mild recession in the period of general growth beginning after 1897. Evidence for a recession in this period does not show up in some annual data series.

1902: UE dip=-16.2%
Though not severe, this downturn lasted for nearly two years and saw a distinct decline in the national product. Industrial and commercial production both declined, albeit fairly modestly. The recession came about a year after a 1901 stock crash.

1907: UE dip=-29.2%
A run on Knickerbocker Trust Company deposits on October 22, 1907, set events in motion that would lead to a severe monetary contraction. The fallout from the panic led to Congress creating the Federal Reserve System.

1910: UE dip=-14.7%

This was a mild but lengthy recession. The national product grew by less than 1%, and commercial activity and industrial activity declined. The period was also marked by deflation.

1914: UE dip=-25.9%

Productions and real income declined during this period and were not offset until the start of World War I increased demand. Incidentally, the Federal Reserve Act was signed during this recession, creating the Federal Reserve System, the culmination of a sequence of events following the Panic of 1907.

1918: UE dip=-24.5%

Severe hyperinflation in Europe took place over production in North America. This was a brief but very sharp recession and was caused by the end of wartime production, along with an influx of labor from returning troops. This, in turn, caused high unemployment.

1920: UE dip=-38.1%
The 1921 recession began a mere 10 months after the post-World War I recession, as the economy continued working through the shift to a peacetime economy. The recession was short, but extremely painful.

1923: UE dip=-25.4%
From the depression of 1920–21 until the Great Depression, an era dubbed the Roaring Twenties, the economy was generally expanding. Industrial production declined in 1923–24, but on the whole this was a mild recession.

In the above data Yitzhak took the liberty to omit the totally nonsensical 1926 recession, for being but a childish revenge on the 1920's harshest critic of EZ, to wit, Henry Ford sr., founder of Ford Motor Company. Since Yitzhak has nothing to conceal to the reader, he hereby fully quotes the website's eliminated row:

1926: UE dip=-10.0%

This was an unusual and mild recession, thought to be caused largely because Henry Ford closed production in his factories for six months to switch from production of the Model T to the Model A. Charles P. Kindleberger says the period from 1925 to the start of the Great Depression is best thought of as a boom, and this minor recession just proof that the boom "was not general, uninterrupted or extensive".

Either the recession was indeed mild, or the GDP and UE dips are exaggerated at last a factor 2. A mild recession *and* 10% unemployment is a contradiction of terms. The quote of Kindleberger emphasizes the contradiction: the boom preceding the Great Depression might have been a financial balloon, and the 1926 recession a short-lived return to normality. Note the cautious but extremely suggestive initial sentence:

"This was an **unusual** and **mild** recession, **thought** to be caused **largely** because Henry Ford closed production in his factories for six months to switch from production of the Model T to the Model A".

I like the 1926 description a lot because it is a typical example of EZ deceit, containing all three usual ingredients:

- the historical reference is true
- the suggestion is self-contradictory: either "it is thought", or "largely", but not both
- the suggestion obviously is a cheap lie, only meant to smearing Henry Ford; the coward revenge on the man who dared publish criticism on the Jewish banking mafia

This sentence fails to mention *who thinks so,* and *to what extent.* As far as the thinking is concerned,[40] the writers of the text surely do not believe a single word of what they write – believing that, is left to the ingenuous.

No recession of the post-World War II era has come anywhere near the depth of the Great Depression. In the Great Depression, GDP fell by 27% (the deepest after demobilization is the recession beginning in December 2007, during which GDP has fallen 5.1% as of the second quarter of 2009) and unemployment rate reached 10% (the highest since was the 10.8% rate reached during the

---

40 The failure of but a single US company (albeit as large as Ford Motor Company) could never have affected a national product by 12%. That would imply that 8 coincident failures (of US companies of Ford's size) would annihilate US' GDP.

1981–82 recession). No recession in the whole world never came anywhere near the depth of the great Depression. Upon disregarding the world-wide influence of US recessions, no single nation on this planet shows a peculiarly strong recession list as that of the US. This is strong evidence for a concerted, non-governmental power, explicitly intent on causing US recessions, specifically financial ones.

1929: UE dip=-22%

A banking panic and a collapse in the money supply took place in the United States. Extensive new tariffs and other factors contributed to an extremely deep depression. GDP, industrial production, employment, and prices fell substantially.

1937: UE dip=-18.0%

This Recession was mainly due to the tight fiscal policy resulting from an attempt to balance the budget after New Deal spending, the tight monetary policy of the Federal Reserve, and the declining profits of businesses led to a reduction in business investment.

1945: UE dip=-5%

The decline in government spending at the end of
World War II led to an enormous drop in gross
domestic product, making this technically a recession.
This was the result of demobilization and the shift
from a wartime to peacetime economy. The post-war
years were unusual in a number of ways
(unemployment was never high) and this era may be
considered a "*sui generis* end-of-the-war recession".

1949: UE dip=8%

The 1948 recession was a brief economic downturn;
forecasters of the time expected much worse,
perhaps influenced by the poor economy in their
recent lifetimes. The recession also followed a period
of monetary tightening.

1953: UE dip=-6%

After a post-Korean War inflationary period, more funds
were transferred to national security. In 1951, the
Federal Reserve reasserted its independence from the
U.S. Treasury and in 1952, the Federal Reserve changed
monetary policy to be more restrictive because of fears
of further inflation or of a bubble forming.

1958: UE dip=7.5%

Monetary policy was tightened during the two years preceding 1957, followed by an easing of policy at the end of 1957. The budget balance resulted in a change in budget surplus of 0.8% of GDP in 1957 to a budget deficit of 0.6% of GDP in 1958, and then to 2.6% of GDP in 1959.

1960: UE dip=-7%

Another primarily monetary recession occurred after the Federal Reserve began raising interest rates in 1959. The government switched from deficit (or 2.6% in 1959) to surplus (of 0.1% in 1960). When the economy emerged from this short recession, it began the second-longest period of growth in NBER history. The Dow Jones Industrial Average (Dow) finally reached its lowest point on Feb. 20, 1961, about 4 weeks after President Kennedy was inaugurated.

2008: UE dip=-10%

The subprime mortgage crisis led to the collapse of the United States housing bubble. Falling housing-related assets contributed to a global financial crisis, even as oil and food prices soared. The crisis led to the failure or collapse of many of the United States' largest financial institutions: Bear Stearns, Fannie Mae, Freddie Mac, Lehman Brothers, Citi Bank and AIG, as well as a crisis in the automobile industry. The government responded with an unprecedented $700 billion bank bailout and $787 billion fiscal stimulus package. The National Bureau of Economic Research declared the end of this recession over a year after the end date. The Dow Jones Industrial Average (Dow) finally reached its lowest point on March 9, 2009.

www.ingramcontent.com/pod-product-compliance
Lightning Source LLC
Chambersburg PA
CBHW071202210326
41597CB00016B/1647